UX

PROGRAMMING

FOR BEGINNERS

Your First Step towards
Creating the Best UI/UX Designs

DYLAN CHRISTIAN

Table of Contents

Introduction

If you have picked up this book, then it is safe to say that you are interested in learning about UX programming. And you have come to the right place! This book will teach you everything you need to know about UX programming, from the basics of what it is to the more advanced concepts.

Each chapter in this book is designed to build upon the knowledge you have learned in the previous chapter. By the end of this book, you will have a strong understanding of what UX programming is and how to apply it to your own designs.

This book is divided into two phases and 10 chapters. Phase 1 is all about learning the basics of UX and UI. We will cover topics such as UX and UI, the different types of UX, how to design user personas according to your UI project, and how to create prototypes. Don't worry; we will go into more detail about what these things mean later. In phase 2, we will be actually doing some practical work. I'll introduce HTML and CSS, and we will be creating a simple e-commerce home page together. Then we will move to a UI Prototype tool that will show us how prototyping works. All the resources are available on our Google drive. I have provided the links so you can download them easily. By the end of this book, you will have a strong understanding of what UX programming is and how to apply it to your own designs.

So without further ado, let's get started!

PHASE 1:
THE BASICS

Chapter 1

Introduction:
What Are UX and UI?

What we'll discuss in this chapter:

- What exactly is UX?

- What is UI?

- What are the basic components of UX?

- What are the basic elements of a UI?

- What do you call a good UX?

- Features of a good UX?

- Why is UX so important in today's world

Design is not just what it looks like or feels like.
Design is how it works -Steve Jobs

You've probably heard the word "User Experience" being thrown here and there. Chances are you are a beginner who wants to learn how UX works. But like many other individuals, you too may have associated it with a very tech-savvy language or some computer language when in reality, it is none of these things. Yes, UX or human-computer interaction is taught as part of many computer sciences courses, but anyone can learn it. ANYONE, including you. Before delving deeper into how you can learn it or why you should learn it, and why it is just so important in today's modern world, let us first discuss what it really is UX.

So, What Is UX?

As you may have guessed by now, UX stands for **User Experience**. See nothing to do with computer science. So why is it called User experience? Well, it means exactly what it sounds; creating a good experience through digital or modern means like mobile phones, tablets, products, services, websites, etc. For the USER, this user experience must be easy, straightforward, responsive, and substantial.

User experience is centered on creating a helpful design that is exactly what the user needs. Even your everyday appliances use UX features such as microwave or oven touchpad interfaces. The same goes for your smart TV. Every human-computer interaction that you come across on any digital or electronic appliance is a user experience for you.

No need to look for the meaning of UX in the outer world. The best way to look for what UX means is through your own experience. You, as the user, may have opened a website or an app. Let's say you want to purchase the new

Nike shoes. So if you opened the Nike website, scrolled around the website, saw the specifications of the product that you wanted to buy, and just had a good look at what you wanted is your own UX (user experience). Congratulations, you had your own User experience via the Nike website, and if this experience was what you were looking for, i.e., easy, straightforward, good navigation, good content, you just had an amazing UX. In fact, that joyful feeling you just had in your gut that's called UX! We, as human beings, are constantly touching or being touched by the world of UX.

Having a mere interface or design is not the goal of UX. This is why having a good UX goes hand in hand with your business or product goal. You need to deliver a seamless, responsive, simple, and straightforward design or solution to the user for them to actually enjoy or like it. That's the sole purpose of making or learning UX in the first place. ***A seamless, excellent experience for the user.***

As I said earlier, UX encompasses product, service, or business.

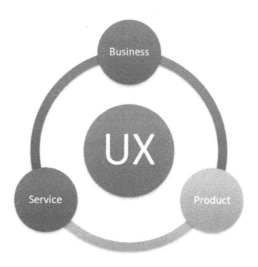

A product isn't made just for its looks or design. It has to function according to its user's or customer's needs. In the universe of product design, UX should be made according to how well the product works.

We're going to tell you the story of a sustainable electronic company called "Electrolux". They are not just about giving high-tech appliances. In fact, they have taken the "interaction" element to a whole new level.
When making their appliances, they pay special attention to user research. Do you know the old adage? To understand what the user needs, you need to walk in their shoes. Well, this is exactly what the design guys do at Electrolux. Taking the example of a dishwasher, good nice research from the company's end revealed that families usually load their dishes during the day and run the dishwater at night. The 2nd thing they noted was that

many individuals opt to choose the quick method to clean their dishes. This was a behavior pattern they noted in most of the homes. They actually did not need the clean dishes quickly.

So, the guys at Electrolux created an interface they named "Quickselect Eco" that takes about 3 hours to finish washing the dishes and takes little energy and water to do the task.

In the end, this User experience resulted in low bills for the families. This is what we call a good UX in product designing and creation.

In building a good User experience design, you must consider the following:

- How easy is it for users to find what they're looking for?

- How easy is it for users to understand what they're seeing?

- How easy is it for users to use the product?

- How satisfying is the overall experience for users?

While we're on the topic of UX, you may have heard about UI, as well. In fact, this little dude gets thrown whenever UX is mentioned. So what is UI?

User interface (UI) is what your users will see when using your product. This includes the buttons, icons, and other visual elements with which they'll interact. Your goal with UI is to make sure that it's easy for your users to understand and use.

A good User interface design must consider the following:

- How easy is it for users to see what they need to see?

- How easy is it for users to interact with the product?

- How intuitive is the design?

- Does the design look good and professional?

Creating a good UX/UI design is all about striking a balance between these two aspects. If you can make your product easy to use and reasonable while also making it look good, you'll be well on your way to creating the best UX/UI designs possible.

Pro Tip:

A tip you need to know when designing a good UX/UI design is to think about how your users will interact with your product. You need to take into account their needs and wants when it comes to using your product. This way, you can design a product that they will love and be able to use easily.

Since UI consists of the visual design of the product, website, tablet, or any medium, here's a list of some of the digital components or elements that make up the user interface:

- Buttons

- Text fields

- Drop-down menus

- Sliders

- Checkboxes

- Radio buttons

- Input fields

- Layout

- CTA (call to action) buttons

- Typography

- Color scheme

- Overall design and aesthetics

Features of UX:

- Good UX must be intuitive and easy to use

- Should be visually appealing

- Must be able to take into account the different ways users might want to use a product

- Needs to have strong problem-solving skills

- Must be able to think creatively

Pro Tip:

UX Industry has set some benchmarks when it comes to what a good UX and UI are. A good user experience will make a product useful, useable, appealing, discoverable, approachable, and reliable. You'll be well-positioned to resume your UX adventure if you hold these qualities in view while you do your investigation.

At this point, I want to show you what a good or bad UX design is. You're all set to make these judgments yourself, but the whole point of the book is to make you able to see and create the best UI/UX design.

Here are some examples of good or bad UI/UX design

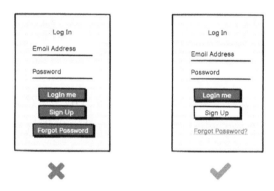

Why is this not a good form? Because you don't need the "forget password" as a button! People need to be taken to a separate link where they can add a new password. So it doesn't have to be a button.

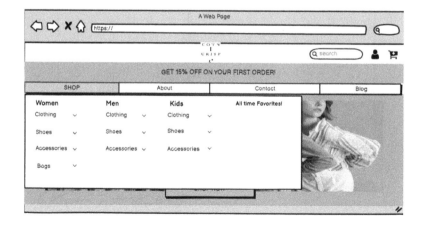

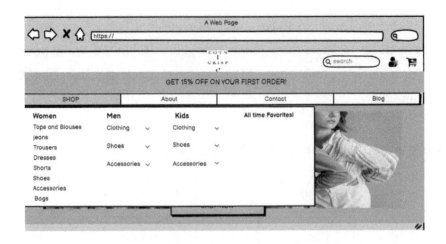

Bad forms make sense, but what is wrong with the above design? If you remember, a key element of an excellent UI is making things easy for the user! See the prototype above; it shows women's clothes and accessories categorized into sections. In contrast, in the 2nd prototype, all the information jumbles together! When making an application, please select a consistent color scheme to follow throughout the website or application.

Again, the login window on the left is quite confusing and bad in terms of UI and UX. You need to correct the user if they entered a wrong [password or prompt them to reset it! In case the user wants to go back or cancel the form, simply add back buttons or a little cancel button at the top left corner. *Give the user a seamless experience.*

Practical Exercise:

Your task for this chapter is to visit mobile applications and websites that you frequently visit and make a list of items or things that you find frustrating and unsatisfying about them. It could be anything from a button that is in the wrong place to a drop-down menu that doesn't work correctly. Once you have a list of things that you find unsatisfying, try to think of ways that they could be improved. This will help you to start thinking like a UX designer.

Remember, you are the user. Do these applications meet your satisfaction? Can you easily operate or use them?

Examples: -Some websites are easy to use and navigate. However, the search function could be improved.

Some Maps/Navigation applications might be easy to use and provides accurate directions. However, the user interface could be improved.

Some Social applications might need help with the overwhelming news feed and can be difficult to keep up with.

If you are unsure where to start, just think about those everyday jobs you do online, such as booking a ticket to the cinema or surfing the internet. Consider how easy or difficult it is to complete these tasks. What could be done to make the experience better? How can you streamline the process?

Some things to keep in mind:

> *-The user should always come first.*

> *-Ease of use is key.*

> *-UX design is about solving problems.*

Jot down these likes and displeasures and list the reasons why you feel so. When you're ready, share your findings with a friend or fellow classmate and see if they have suggestions for improving the experience.

Chapter 2

Some Basic UX & UI Components You Need to Know

Outline of this chapter:

- What are the components of the UX?

- Basic components of the UX

- Key components of the UX

- What are the components of the UI?

- Practical task

A user interface is like a joke. If you have to explain it, it is not that good. - Martin LeBlanc.

User experience and user interface are very important for any website to work. Without these two elements, even the best website is doomed to fail.

If you own a business, you know how important it is to make a user-friendly website that will give you a competitive edge.

Because, let's be honest, you can't afford to invest in a website that's hard to use and cluttered with unnecessary content.

In this section, we have all the important bits covered for you. You know what UX and UI are. You know all the basics. It is time to get serious about UI/UX and just get in there, you know. In this chapter, you will be looking at the elements that make up the website and mobile applications, such as Buttons, logos, search bar, etc. You may have heard about these elements, but trust me when I say they have the power to build your UX design or may destroy it altogether. Designed the wrong button? Forgot to put a search bar? Yup, there goes your website in the pit of all failed websites. So, let's jump right into it. Not the pit. The chapter.

What Are the Components of UX?

When we talk about the user experience, we may talk about two different types of components:

1. Basic components

2. Key components

Basic components	Key components
Usefulness	User Research
Desirability	UX Strategy

Accessibility	UX Design
Credibility	UX Testing
Findability	
Value	
Usability	

Basic Components of the UX

The following are the basic components of the user Experience:

- **Usefulness**

It is a really important component of your website, mobile application, or product. The more useful your website/product/app is, the more effective it will be. You don't want to put your website online with useless information. It will be useless to your customers. To avoid that, ensure the website's content is useful to your customers. Make sure that your content is interesting and helpful to your customers. When your customers visit your website, they should have a good time reading your content.

A great example of usefulness is Google's search engine. It is easy to use and understand, and it is effective at helping users find the information they are looking for.

- **Desirability**

The desirability component of UX is about whether a product has been designed in a way that makes people want to use it. It is one of the important factors in making sure people use your product. The desirability component of UX should be considered carefully.

Pro Tip:

How to make users want your product? The first step to making users want your product is to understand what they desire. This can be done by conducting user research. User research is a process that involves observing and interviewing users to learn about their needs and desires. Once you understand what users desire, you can create designs that address those needs and desires. It is also important to create an emotional connection with the user. This can be done by creating designs that are visually appealing and making use of color, typography, and other graphical elements in an effective way. Another way to create an emotional connection with the user is to tell a story through the design. For example, a website's home page could tell the company's story and how it started. In conclusion, to make users want your product, you must understand what they desire and create designs that address those needs and desires. You should also create an emotional connection with the user by creating visually appealing designs that tell a story.

- **Accessibility**

Accessibility means making sure everyone can use your product. When designing a product, it is important to keep in mind that not everyone has the same ability to use it. For example, some people may have difficulty using a mouse or keyboard, while others may be blind or have low vision. There are many different ways to make a product accessible. These include adding alternative text to images, adding captions to videos, and effectively using color and contrast. By keeping accessibility in mind when designing a product, you can ensure that everyone can use it.

- **Credibility**

Credibility means making sure users trust your product. When designing a product, it is important to remember that users need to trust the product to use it. There are many different ways to build trust with users. Some of these include using credible sources, providing privacy and security, and offering customer support. Keeping credibility in mind when designing a product can ensure that users will trust it.

Amazon is an example of a company that has built trust with its users. Amazon is an online retailer that offers a wide variety of products. The website is easy to use and provides a secure checkout process. In addition, Amazon offers customer support in case there are any problems with an order.

A case study of usefulness, usability, and aesthetics is Facebook. Facebook is a social networking website that allows users to connect with friends and family. The website is easy to use and understand, and it is effective at helping the user stay connected with their friends and family. The website is also visually appealing and uses color, typography, and other graphical elements in an effective way. In conclusion, UI/UX designers must keep in mind that the designs they create must be useful, usable, and aesthetically pleasing. By doing so, they will create designs that are effective at helping the user achieve their goals.

- **Findability**

The findability component of the user experience refers to the ability of users to locate and find information on the web quickly. A useful, easily accessible website is easy to navigate and has a clean, simple design. Search engines such as Google use the findability component as one of their main criteria for ranking websites. If a page doesn't rank highly, it may have other problems, but poor findability can cause a page to rank low regardless of whether it has other problems.

- **Value**

The value of user experience cannot be defined. It is something that can only be experienced by using it. The product team's goal is to ensure that the user experience is valuable. The process of designing and developing a product involves looking into several aspects of the product.

For example, people do not buy new clothes because they think that they are fashion-forward. They buy them because they believe they look good. They do this just to increase their value. In this way, value is necessary for the UX too.

*You probably do not hear too much about it. Let us just say it once and for all; **make sure your product/service or UX is worth the user's time**. When designing a product, website, or application, it is important to remember that users need to feel like the product is worth their time. There are many ways to add value to a product or experience.*

> *Some of these include providing useful features, making the product easy to use, and offering a good customer experience. By keeping value in mind when designing a product, you can ensure that users will feel like it is worth their time. One example of a company that has added value to its product is Google Maps. Google Maps is a web mapping service that provides directions and maps for various locations. The website is easy to use and provides accurate directions. In addition, Google Maps offers a variety of features such as satellite view and traffic conditions.*

- **Usability**

A website's usability is the ease with which users can interact with its content and navigate through it. The more accessible a website is, the more useful it is for the audience. In a digital world, people expect websites to work properly. Users can only accept websites that work. For this reason, usability is a quite important factor in UX.

Pro tip:

What are some ways you can ensure your product is usable? There are many different ways to make sure your product is usable. Some of these include making the product easy to use, providing clear instructions, and offering customer support.

The Crux of UX Basic Components

Usefulness	Talks about how a site's audience might benefit from it
Desirability	Talk about what your audience wants, whether or not they want your website or items.
Accessibility	Talks about the need to make the website's UI accessible to everyone since if people can't utilize it, they won't reap its benefits
Credibility	Talks about how the users should have faith in your interface and believe that the information you provide is trustworthy

Findability	Talks about the user's ability to rapidly find information online
Value	Talks about the product team's goal of ensuring a valuable customer experience
Usability	Talks about the website's content and navigation ease

Key Components of UX

Many different aspects make up the field of user experience, from research and strategy to design and testing. But what exactly are the key components of UX? Here's a quick rundown:

1. **User Research**

The first step in any good UX process is understanding your users and their needs. This can be done through various research methods, such as interviews, surveys, focus groups, and user testing.

A great example of user research is the case study done by Dropbox. Dropbox is a file sharing and storage service that allows users to store their files in the cloud. The company conducted user research to understand how users were using their product. Based on the findings, Dropbox made changes to the design of its website and apps. These changes helped to improve the user experience and make it easier for users to share and store their files

2. UX Strategy

Once you have a solid understanding of your users, you need to set some goals and objectives for your design. This is where UX strategy comes in. It's all about figuring out what your users need and want from your product or service and then creating a plan to deliver it.

3. UX Design

This is the fun part! Once you have your strategy in place, it's time to start designing the actual user experience. This includes everything from wireframing and prototyping to visual design and usability testing.

4. UX Testing

No matter how well you think you've designed your product, there's always room for improvement. That's where UX testing comes in. You can get feedback on what's working well and what needs to be changed by running various tests with real users.

So there you have it! These are the four key components of UX. Of course, there's a lot more to it than just these four things, but if you can master these basics, you're well on your way to creating great user experiences.

The Crux of UX Key Components

User Research	For research purposes, interviews, surveys, focus groups, and user testing are done
UX Strategy	It's all about figuring out what your users need and want and then delivering it
UX Design	Wireframing, prototyping, graphic design, and usability testing are included in this step
UX Testing	In this step, by testing with real users, you can learn what's working and what needs changing

What Are the Elements of the UI?

Elements of a user interface are typically classified as belonging to one of these four categories:

1. *Input Controls*

Input controls are the elements that allow the user to interact with the interface. This can include buttons, icons, and input fields.

The following are some of the input controls:

- Checkboxes

- Radio buttons

- Dropdown lists

- List boxes

- Buttons

- Toggles

- Text fields

- Input field

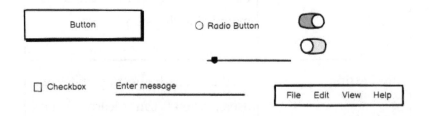

2. Navigation Components

The navigational components of UI are the elements that allow users to move around within the interface. This can include things like menus, buttons, and links. These elements help users to find their way around the interface and to access the features and information they need.

Breadcrumb navigation

Shop › About › Contact › **Blog ›**

Navigation Components of UI are:

- Top Navigation
- Bottom Navigation
- Side Navigation
- Search Bar

Top Navigation – A navigation bar at the top of a screen.

- It is used in case the screen does not have a scroll bar.
- The top navigation typically includes a search bar or menu options for the user to select.

Bottom Navigation – A navigation bar at the bottom of the screen

- It is used in case the screen does not have a navigation bar.

Side Navigation – A navigation bar at the side of the screen.

- This navigation is usually available in web browsers only.

3. *Informational Components*

Informational components of UI typically include elements like labels, text fields, and buttons that provide users with information about what they can do within the interface. This UI element is important in helping users understand how to use the interface and navigate its various features. Without these informational components, users would likely be lost and frustrated when trying to use the interface.

There are four main informational components of UI:

- Labels are the text that appears on the screen to help users understand what they're looking at or what they need to do. They should be clear, concise, and easy to read.

Amazon   Add to cart   Add User   Address Book   Contrast Adjust

Ambulance   Android   App.net   File archive   Behance

- Icons are small graphical images that represent something on the screen. They can be used to represent a function or to provide visual cues to help users navigate.

- Input fields are where users enter information into the website or app. They should be easy to find and use and should provide clear instructions on what kind of information is needed.

- Buttons are the clickable elements that allow users to take action within the UI. They should be easily visible and clearly labeled so that users know what they do.

When designing your UI, keeping these four informational components in mind is important. By making sure that your UI is well-designed and informative, you can help users easily navigate your content.

4. Layout

Layout refers to the arrangement of elements on a page. The layout can be used to create a consistent look and feel throughout your designs.

The Crux of UI Components

Input controls	Input control lets users change the UI state. This could entail updating text font, button image, menu item content, or introducing a new menu item.
Navigation components	UI navigational elements let users navigate the interface. Menus, buttons, and links are examples. These elements assist users in navigating and accessing features and information. • Top navigation • Bottom navigation • Side navigation
Informational components	Labels, text fields, and buttons provide users with information about the interface. This sort of UI element helps users traverse the interface's functionality.
Layout	The arrangement of elements on a page

Practical Work

Open a few websites and see which websites have been created by making use of these UI and UX components and elements and which have not. See the difference between a well-designed website and a poorly designed one. Try to find out the reason for this difference. From your observations, make a list of Do's and Don'ts for a good website design. What would you do differently if you were to design a website? Then, compare the results, take note of any differences, and talk with your colleagues about how the underperforming sites might be improved.

Remember: When creating any kind of user experience or user interface, make sure to keep the main points of this chapter in mind.

Chapter 3

UI and UX Design
Processes and Methods

Outline of this chapter:

- What is the UI design process?

- What is the UX design process?

- Different methods to conduct User Interface Research

- The key phases of UX

- Methods to create UI

- Design thinking

> *When UX doesn't consider all USERS, shouldn't it be*
> *known as "SOME user experience or...SUX? "*
> *-Billy Gregory*

You know a great deal about UI and UX at this stage. You know all the little details, but still, we're far from calling ourselves *UI designers*. There is still a lot you need to know before jumping to actually writing UI codes. Like every creation or invention has a starting point, the same goes for a UI design. UX and UI follow a design process or pattern actually to be able to work. Since the *user* is the center of both of these universes, you need to do hefty research on the user of your product. For this purpose, we will be taking things to another level in this chapter.

What Processes Are Involved in Creating a UI Design?

The UI design process is all about creating products that are **easy to use**. This means that UI designers need to have a strong understanding of how users interact with products. They also need to be able to take into account the different ways that users might want to use a product.

To create a good UI, designers must have a good programming understanding. This is because they need to be able to code the functionality of the product. We will come to the programming later on. For now, let us just concentrate on the basics of UI/UX.

Now, remember when we said UI and UX are all about creating something for a particular user? This means you'll have to do research on gathering this information.

Many different methods can be used to conduct UI research. Some common methods include

- Interviews.
- Surveys.
- Focus groups.

- User testing.

UI designers need to be able to choose the right method for each project. They also need to interpret the data they collect and use it to improve the product.

If you're looking for a good online survey tool to carry out your survey regarding user research, you can try Survey Monkey (https://www.surveymonkey.com/) and Typeform (typeform.com)

As I mentioned above, there is a criterion to starting everything. It would be best if you had a roadmap in front of you to be able to tread carefully on what you want to do. Without a roadmap or framework, or process, you will get lost. For this purpose, UX geniuses have introduced some key phases to start the UX design process.

UX has 3 Key Phases

1. *Discovery:*

The discovery phase is about understanding the problem you are trying to solve. This means that you need to do research in order to understand the needs of the users. You also need to understand the business goals of the product. This phase can be broken down into 4 sub-phases:

- **Problem definition:**

In this phase, you will define the problem that you are trying to solve. This means that you will need to identify the users' needs and the product's business goals.

- **Research:**

In this phase, you will conduct research to understand the needs of the users. This research can be conducted through interviews, surveys, focus groups, and user testing.

- **Analysis:**

In this phase, you will analyze the data that you collected in the research phase. This analysis will help you to understand the needs of the users.

- **Solution:**

In this phase, you will define the solution to the problem that you specified in the problem definition phase. This solution will be based on the users' needs and the product's business goals.

2. Design:

The design phase is about creating a solution that meets the users' needs. This means that you need to design a product that is easy to use and meets the product's business goals. This phase can be broken down into 4 sub-phases:

- **Information Architecture:**

In this phase, you will define the structure of the product. This includes defining the pages, navigation, and content.

- **Interaction Design:**

In this phase, you will define how the users will interact with the product. This includes defining the user flow and the user interface.

- **Visual Design:**

In this phase, you will define the look and feel of the product. This includes choosing colors, typography, and images.

- **Prototyping:**

In this phase, you will create a prototype of the product. This prototype will be used to test the usability of the product.

3. Development:

The development phase is all about turning the design into a working product. This means you must code and test the product to ensure it works correctly. This phase can be broken down into 4 sub-phases:

- **Coding:**

In this phase, you will code the product. This includes writing the HTML, CSS, and JavaScript.

- **Testing:**

In this phase, you will test the product to ensure it works correctly. This testing can be conducted through user testing or A/B testing.

- **Deployment:**

In this phase, you will deploy the product to a server. This will make the product available to users.

- **Maintenance:**

In this phase, you will maintain the product. This includes fixing bugs and adding new features.

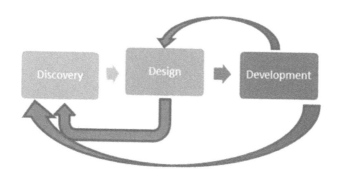

In real life, you don't always go smoothly from step 1 to step 2 and step 3. There are repetitive iterations in every step. Perhaps in design face, you'll feel the need to go back to the discovery face. Perhaps in the development phase, you'll need to return to the design face if there is some problem in coding.

> *Business goals and product goals go hand in hand. The user experience is the way a person feels when using a product. This includes everything from how easy it is to use the product to how satisfied they are with the results. A good UX design must consider the needs of the users and the product's business goals. Creating a good UX design involves four phases: discovery, design, development, and maintenance. Each phase has its own set of activities that need to be completed in order to create a successful product. You also need to understand the business goals of the product.*

A good UI designer must keep these stages in mind. You need to be patient. Okay, here's the amazing part of this chapter. The part that will actually make you feel like yes! You are doing something good! Because now, we are going to discuss how designers create their first designs- or as we call them in UI language-*Mockups* or prototypes!

Some methods to create UI are:

1- **Wireframing**: A wireframe is a low-fidelity mockup of a product. This means that it is a sketch of the product that includes its basic layout and structure. Wireframes are used to create a starting point for the design process. Below is an image of a wireframe of a registration process of a mobile App.

2- **Prototyping**: A prototype is a working model of a product. This means that it is a version of the product that can be used to test its usability of the product. Prototypes are used to gather feedback on the design of the product.

3- **User testing**: User testing is a method of testing a product with actual users. This gives you feedback on how the product works in the real world. User testing can be done with paper prototypes or with working prototypes.

4- **A/B testing**: A/B testing is a method of testing two different versions of a product to see which one performs better. This is done by creating two versions of the product and then testing them with users. The version that performs better is used as the final product.

5- **Maintenance**: Maintenance is all about keeping the product up-to-date. This means that you need to fix any bugs and add new features as needed. Maintenance also includes making sure that the product works with new devices and software.

As you can see, a lot goes into creating a good UX design. If you want to create the best UX designs, you need to understand all the phases of the process and the methods used. You also need to have a strong understanding of the users' needs and the product's business goals. If you are new to UX design, taking a course or reading a book on the subject can be helpful. There are many great resources out there that will teach you everything you need to know about UX design. Once you have a strong understanding of the basics, you can start to create your own designs.

Woohoo, it was not that difficult, was it? And look at you, with your knowledge of wireframes and prototypes and stuff you didn't t know a month ago! Almost every field of life and every activity is created or begins with an idea with a thought. There's a process to everything. On a Sunday morning, even though you were planning to wake up late, you remembered that you had to get eggs and bread from the supermarket before your wife and kids woke up. Because if you're late, it will take 20 minutes to get these things, by which the kids will be crying, and the wide will be angry. So what do you do? You get in your car, go to the nearest supermarket and buy those eggs! But

you don't feel like doing all of this. It is Sunday, after all!
So you give the car keys to your help and ask him to fetch
you your eggs and bread! See? This was design thinking in
everyday life. You understood the users' needs, saw the
problem, and came up with a solution!

What Is Design Thinking in UI/UX?

Design thinking is a problem-solving method used to create innovative solutions. This method is typically used in the fields of design and engineering. However, it can also be used in other fields, such as business and education. Design thinking is about understanding the user's needs and creating a solution that meets those needs.

The design thinking process includes four main steps:
empathize, define, ideate, and prototype. These steps are
designed to help you understand the problem, develop
creative solutions, and test those solutions. If you want to
learn more about design thinking, many great resources
are available. You can find books, articles, and courses on
the subject. You can also attend workshops or conferences
where you can learn

There are 5 keys to design thinking, and you can apply them to your everyday life like the example I gave above:

1. **Empathize with your User**: In order to design a solution, you need to understand the problem. This means that you

need to put yourself in the user's shoes and understand their needs.

2. **Define the problem**: Once you understand the problem, you need to define it. This will help you come up with a clear goal for your design.

3. **Ideate**: This is the stage where you come up with creative solutions to the problem. This is done by brainstorming or using other creative methods.

4. **Prototype**: A prototype is a working model of your solution. This helps you test your idea and see if it works in the real world.

5. **Test**: Once you have a prototype, you need to test it with users. This will give you feedback on your design and help you improve it. Design thinking is a powerful tool that can help you solve problems in your everyday life. Using the five steps of design thinking, you can come up with innovative solutions to any problem.

A Non-linear process:
Like The phases of UX, design thinking doesn't follow a linear or straight pattern. In real life, many different teams are working on product development. They constantly go back to earlier stages whenever they find new insight about the product. Each team in the design department is working simultaneously with each other.

Practical Work:

Get ready because you're going to take your first step into becoming a UX/UI designer and creating your first mockup!

By now, you know what UI elements are and what components or points you need to keep in mind to make the UX flow seamless! For this exercise, we'll create a website's home page! We will take this exercise into phase two of the book, where we'll actually look at some UI/UX coding via CSS and HTML!

But before that coding, we have quite a journey to cover! At this stage, you don't even need a tool. Just grab a paper and pencil and start designing what the home page should look like. You can take help from the UI elements we have listed in chapter 2 or can search for your own.

Why pen and paper sketch? You'll be astonished to know that many top-notch designers use paper prototyping as the first step in creating a design. You only need a pencil and some paper to get off. We'll make a wireframe of a website and demonstrate how it enables a fast, adaptive creative process. Doing this will produce ongoing data that you may use for both yourself and a customer. Additionally, you can use this to rationalize your strategy prior to spending any time actually programming it.

Now, as a user, whenever you open a website, you are first met with a home page, right? It is the main page. It has the main content in it. The page basically tells you at first glance what the site is about.

It has a sidebar to help you navigate or may have a navigation bar. It may have a search field, the main header image that slides and some other features.

Here's my take on a simple Ecommerce Homepage

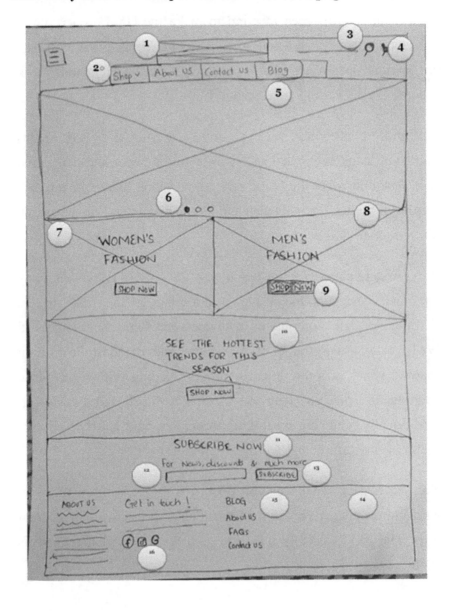

1. I have made a little *logo* here. It's imperative but not necessary to mention your company or brand's logo.

2. Now, this bar is called the "*Navigation bar*", as you already know. You can click on any of the buttons to navigate to pages of your choice. Many home pages have these navigation bars.

3. *Search bar*: You'll also find the search bar at the top left corner of many websites.

4. Since this is a product or eCommerce home page, I have also shown a product cart. When you add a product to your cart, you'll see a number pop up on the cart that'll show you the number of items in your cart. Trust us; this is also a good UX design.

5. Header Image: This is the main image on the home page. It basically demonstrates what the website is about. In our case, it would show men's or women's fashion items.

6. See those little dots? They show that this image is a slider image. Many developers and designers use image sliders. The dark or highlighted dot shows the current slide is showing.

7. Now I have added a separate block showing women's fashion since you see this entity on most eCommerce pages.

8. Similarly, I have a separate image showing men's fashion as well.

9. Both of these separate images have their own buttons that will take the user to these separate categories of fashion.

10. Again I have another image/entity showing the season's latest trends. This will take you to the popular items on this site. These items are sorted separately because they are the most bought.

11. We have a subscribe section, which I think is important if you are a customer looking for regular updates.

12. We have an input field where you'll type your email address

13. Subscribe button.

14. This section is called the footer. Many home pages or landing pages have this section.

15. We have links to take you to any page you want to go from the current home page.

16. Some social media links of the brand.

Chapter 4

Information Architecture

Outline of this chapter:

- Content in UI/UX

- Type of content

- Information Architecture in UX/UI

- common information architecture techniques

- Sitemap

- Practical Task

> *Design in the absence of content is not design, its*
> *decoration.-Jeffrey Zeldman*

Yup, we're getting there. I'm sure at this point. You feel you know everything about UI and UX. I would feel the same after going through this much knowledge. And kudos, you have also started working on making your first wireframes! Well, the good news is we have more fun activities in this chapter as well. So keep reading. And it just keeps getting better and better.

Okay, so now that you know all the fat words and the who's-who of UI and UX, let's discuss the big technical things now. Let's discuss what UX and UI are actually made up of, and how to actually begin working on UI and UX.

Content isn't brought up much when we talk about UI or UX. However, it is as important as the design. Just like the quote above, content really is everything. Many businesses today employ content writers to develop their content and provide visitors and customers with greater value. Our purpose can be communicated through content. From a content and UX viewpoint, it is crucial to have a strategy for bridging customer and organizational objectives. It offers a clear knowledge of what we must do (the kind of material that connects to people and meets their requirements) and how we can do it.

Content Management in UX/UI

User experience is not only about the design of your website or app. It is also about the content on your site. Content is the information that is displayed on your site. This includes text, images, videos, and anything else users can see. Content needs to be well-written and accurate. It also needs to be relevant to the user. Content should be easy to read and understand. It should also be easy to find. The way that content is organized on your site can have a big impact on the user experience. This is why it is important to have a good understanding of content.

There are many different types of content, each with its purpose. Here are some of the most common types of content:

- **Text**: Text is the most common type of content. It is used to provide information to users.

- **Images**: Images are used to add visual interest to your site. They can also be used to provide information to users.

- **Videos**: Videos are a great way to add interest to your site. They can also be used to provide information to users.

- **Audio**: Audio can be used to add interest to your site. It can also be used to provide information to users.

- **Animations**: Animations can be used to add interest to your site. They can also be used to provide information to users.

Content needs to be well-written and accurate. It also needs to be relevant to the user. Content should be easy to read and understand. It should also be easy to find. The way that content is organized on your site can have a big impact on the user experience. This is why it is important to have a good understanding of content.

It's imperative to note some content terms here because I'll be throwing them a lot in the mixture.

1. **Primary Content**: In short, this content must be on the front of your website and have the most visibility. This content is the most important to the user. An example of

primary content is a headline. Since we're dealing with the UI/UX universe, the content you see on the main home page without scrolling is the primary content.

2. **Secondary content**: secondary content is less important to the user and doesn't need to be shown on the upper portion of the home page. Most content writers write secondary content below the fold (visible after scrolling).

3. **Tertiary Content**: Least important o the user, and they usually actively search for it. An example of tertiary content is a social media b

Well, there you go. You know the essential terms and facts regarding content management.

Ever wonder why some websites are plain boring? Why do they have less web traffic? The answer is simple. It is because of their content. Some common problems with content are:

- It is not well-written, making it difficult for users to understand.

- It is not relevant: This can make it difficult for users to find the information they are looking for.

- It is not easy to find: This can make it difficult for users to find the information they are looking for.

- It is not accurate: This can lead to misinformation.

- It is not up-to-date: This can make it difficult for users to find the information they are looking for.

According to a survey by the Content Marketing Institute, nearly 60% of B2B marketers said they plan to produce more content in 2017 than they did in 2016. The pressure is to create quality content that grabs attention and converts customers. But with so much online information, how can you make sure your content stands out? One way to ensure your content is easy to find and use is to focus on information architecture.

Now that you know that a website isn't just buttons and panels and navigation, the content is also an important part of it, if not the most important. When writing content, you need to follow a structure. You can't just randomly put content here and there. It has to be properly organized and should be put in place relevant for its use, and should be easily accessible to the user. This is called information architecture and is an important component of designing platforms. Let's learn a bit more about Information architecture.

Information Architecture in UX/UI

When it comes to creating a great user experience, information architecture is one of the most important aspects. Information architecture is the process of organizing and labeling the content on your website or app. This is important because it helps users find the information they are looking for. There are many different ways to organize information. An example of information architecture can be seen in the way a website is structured. The home page typically contains links to the most important pages on the site.

From there, users can navigate to other pages by clicking on links. The website's structure makes it easy for users to find the content they need.

What are Some Common Information Architecture Techniques?

The most common method is to use a **hierarchical structure**. This means that the most important information is at the top of the hierarchy, and the less critical data is lower.

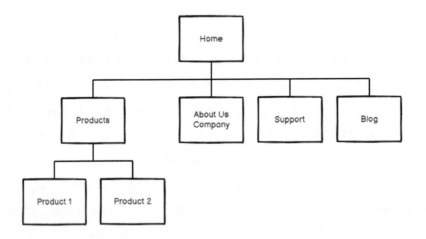

Another standard method is to use a **card sort**. This is where you create cards with different pieces of information on them. The user then sorts the cards into different categories. This can help you to understand how users think about the information on your site.

How Can Information Architecture Be Used to Improve the User Experience?

Information architecture can be used to improve the user experience by making it easier for users to find and use the content they need. Good information architecture makes products more enjoyable to use and helps users achieve their goals. An example of how information architecture can be used to improve the user experience is by creating a clear and easy-to-use navigation system.

Sitemap:

Think of the sitemap as no more than a map of your city. Just like a map, a sitemap shows different pathways, structures and maps of the entire website or application.

It can help you understand how users will flow through your site and what pages are most important. Creating a sitemap is one of the first steps in information architecture. It allows you to see your website as a whole and identify any areas that may need improvement. Once you have created a sitemap, you can use it to create a website navigation system. A well-designed navigation system will help users find the content they need without difficulty. Additionally, a good navigation system will be consistent across all website pages, which will allow users to know where they are on the website.

A sitemap typically contains a list of all the pages on the site and their hierarchy. This tool can help determine the website's structure and how the pages should be linked together.

Remember card sorting? It is a tremendous Site mapping tool. Why? Well, let us see. If you need to sort out and organize your website pages, you can quickly sort or organize these pages into groups. You can provide your design team with cards of different pages and tell them to sort them into relevant groups. Don't worry if you don't understand these things now; we have an activity at the end.

It is crucial to keep the user experience in mind when designing a website. Information architecture is one way to do this by making it easy for users to find and use the content they need. By following some common information architecture principles and using tools such as sitemaps, card sorting, and tree testing, you can create a well-structured website that will improve the user experience. If you're looking for an example of a good sitemap, look no further than the home page of Smashing Magazine.

This popular web design blog uses a simple yet effective sitemap to help users find the content they need. The sitemap is clearly labeled and easy to navigate. Additionally, the sitemap is consistent on all site pages, which helps users know where they are in the product at all times. Smashing Magazine's sitemap is an excellent example of how information architecture can be used to improve the user experience

Practical Work

We have exciting practical work for you. I'm sure you can't help but jump right into making your first UI/UX design. And since you know quite a lot of facts and information about building UX design, let's level up our UX design game. In this exercise, we will be building a sitemap! For this purpose, I need you to see some websites, see their pages and content and make a list of the main pages, categories, and sub-categories. For this exercise, we will continue the activity from the previous chapter, where we made an eCommerce website. Putting that prototype into perspective, here's a sitemap that I built.

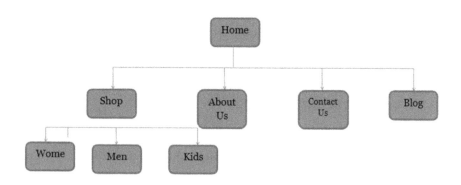

The first level is the **primary content** of the e-commerce website. I have illustrated the level 1 or primary content pages: shop, about us, contact us, and blog. Level 2 or secondary content stage has also been shown but not in detail. The shop page gives pathways to women, men, and kids pages. As your sitemap progresses, you'll add more ages and develop more pathways. You will probably change the names or add or delete some pages. But for starters, this is how a sitemap is created.

This sitemap is a classic example of how designers make an Ecommerce website. Now let's explain each page:

1. **Shop**: It is natural to have a shop us or shop page or placeholder on the main home page of any eCommerce website. You see it immediately on the top navigation bar. This is the primary content and will most likely be on every page. This pathway will most likely produce categories such as women's, men's, and kids' fashion, as well as top trending pieces.

2. **About us**: Like every business and website, this eCommerce shop too has an about us page where users and visitors can find information about the brand.

3. **Contact Us**: If the visitor or user wants to find any information related to the brand, they can go to this page. They'll most likely find the company's contact number and media links here.

4. **Blog**: A blog can add value to this business as it can help visitors highlight content around the fashion world. Blogs

are a great way to make up your mind regarding purchasing behavior.

So this is your primary content. You are on your way to creating an information architecture. You can keep adding pages to this level 1 and make pathways to other pages of the website.

I have made a pathway that extends through the shop category.

Creating New Pathways:

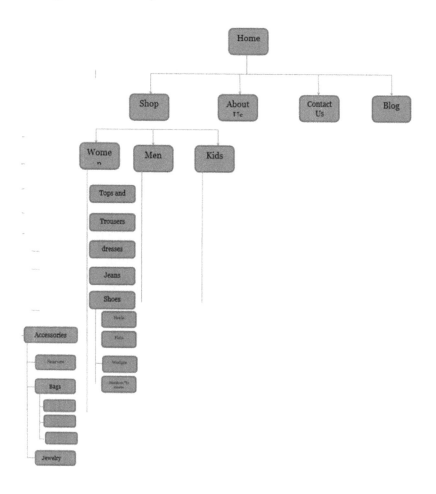

1. **Level 2**: You are met with different categories as you click the shop page or go to the shop page. Since you can either shop for women's fashion, men's fashion, or kid's fashion, we have made these three categories. This is level 2 of the site map. As you can see, new browsing pathways are opening up from the home page.

2. **Level 3**: Level 3 further consists of more items regarding women's fashion. These sub-categories include Tops and blouses, pants, jeans, trousers, and dresses. A good designer will add additional items into these categories. For example, you can make three sub-categories or product pages of the dresses page. After all, there are many different types of dresses.

So, in a nutshell, this is the blueprint for creating a sitemap. It's a fun activity but a tiring one and a complicated one. So your task is to add further sub-categories and product pages to the rest of the placeholders. Need help? Regarding the "About Us" page, think about what further information a company can add. It doesn't have to be a separate page. You can add secondary or tertiary content as well. I think "What we do?" and "Who are we?" are two essential pieces of information a company should show on their about bus page. Why don't you create these levels and add this relevant information to the sitemap above?

Chapter 5

Visual Designing

Outline of this chapter:

- What is visual design?

- Principles of Visual Design.

- Graphic Designing VS Visual Designing

- core components of Visual Design:

- style guide

- Core components of a style guide

This chapter is going to be very interesting. For one thing, you will resonate with it the most of all chapters because visuals are what you see when you use an app or visit a website. It's the most appealing aspect of UI/UX. And quite frankly, it is probably, for many designers, the most exciting part. Creating visuals is actually a fun activity. So in this chapter, we will be discussing visual design in UX.

What Is Visual Design in UX?

Visual design in UX is all about creating user interfaces that are both **effective** and **appealing** to users. It involves a deep understanding of how users interact with digital products and using that knowledge to create designs that meet their needs. Although it is often used interchangeably with User Experience (UX) design, Visual design is a more specific field that focuses on the *look* and *feel* of a product. Visual designers are responsible for creating the overall aesthetic of a product and ensuring that it is both visually appealing and easy to use.

A Good visual design makes products *easier to use* and more *enjoyable* to interact with. It can also help communicate your brand's identity and make complex information more digestible.

Visual design has many different aspects, but some of the most important elements include *typography*, *color*, *iconography*, and *layout*. When used effectively, these elements can come together to create beautiful, intuitive, and user-friendly interfaces.

We recommend checking out some online courses if you're interested in pursuing a career in visual design or are simply curious to learn more about what it entails. They cover everything from the basics of design principles to more advanced topics like working with grid systems and animation.

People tend to think that visual design is all about making things "*look pretty.*" But there's much more to it than that. You may have heard of the *Aesthetic-usability* effect, and it's a theory that suggests that people will perceive more attractive designs as being more user-friendly. This means that if you want your product to be seen as easy to use, you need to make sure it has a great visual design. For example, Apple is known for its beautiful products and user-friendly interfaces. This isn't a coincidence—their visual design choices make their products more enjoyable and easier to use, which in turn makes people more likely to continue using them.

While the Aesthetic-usability effect is a real phenomenon, it's important to remember that visual design is about more than just making things look good. Effective visual design must also take into account the user's needs and the overall goal of the product. A beautiful product that's difficult to use will not be successful, no matter how pretty it looks.

Although the *wireframes* and *prototypes* created by UX designers provide the foundation for a product's visual design, Visual designs give the actual meaning to a product or service. In the eyes of the user, Visual design is what makes a product beautiful, easy to use, and ultimately successful.

Simply put, Visual design is what makes a product look good in the eyes of its target users. It is indeed a user experience created only for the eyes of its targeted users. Wireframes, prototypes, layouts, sitemaps, etc., are just one aspect of the UX universe. Visual design gives life to these aspects.

So how do you get started with visual designing? Well, first, you need to understand the basics of design principles. Visual design is all about creating designs that are both visually appealing and easy to use. To do this, designers must take into account the user's needs and the overall goal of the product when creating their designs. Additionally, Visual designers must pay attention to detail in order to create beautiful and user-friendly designs.

There are several basic design principles that all Visual designers should keep in mind:

- **Balance**: Balance is the distribution of visual weight within a design. There are three types of balance: symmetrical, asymmetrical, and radial.

- **Contrast**: Contrast is the difference between two colors or two elements. Good contrast makes elements easier to see and understand(you will understand it much better once you view our website displayed at the end of this chapter)

Copyright © Author

Hierarchy: Hierarchy is the arrangement of elements in a design from most important to least important. Good hierarchy makes it easy for users to understand the purpose of a design.

Graphic Designing vs. Visual Designing

Graphic design and visual design are often confused because they both deal with the visual aspect of a product or service. However, there is a big difference between the two disciplines. Graphic design is about creating visuals that communicate a message, while visual design is about visually appealing and user-friendly visuals. They both require a deep understanding of how users interact with digital products. Still, Visual designers must also consider the product's overall goal when creating their designs.

A good example of this is the difference between a website's homepage and its product page. A website's homepage needs to be visually appealing to attract users, but its product page needs to be user-friendly to convert users.

In the early days of the internet, there was a website called Geocities. It was one of the first web hosting companies, allowing users to create their own websites. The problem with Geocities was that it allowed users to create any website they wanted without regard for design principles. As a result, many of the websites created on Geocities were chaotic, cluttered, and difficult to use. In 2009, Yahoo! bought Geocities and decided to redesign the website from scratch. They hired a visual design firm, SY Partners, to help with the redesign.

The designers at SY Partners knew that in order to create a successful redesign, they needed to focus on creating a user-friendly interface. They also wanted to make sure that the website was visually appealing, so they used a variety of colors and images to create a fun and inviting design. The redesign was a success, and Geocities is now one of the world's most popular web hosting companies.

In 2012, the Olympic Games were held in London. The organizers of the games wanted to create a visual identity that would be used on all of the signage and branding for the event. They hired a graphic design firm, Wolff Olins, to create the visual identity.

Wolff Olins knew they needed to create an identity that was unique and recognizable. They also wanted it to be simple enough that it could be used on a variety of different materials. After much experimentation, they settled on a design that was inspired by the Union Jack flag. The resulting visual identity was a huge success, and it helped to make the 2012 Olympic Games one of the most memorable and successful events in history.

So, there you have it! Those are just a few examples of the difference between graphic design and visual design. As you can see, both disciplines are important, but they serve different purposes. If you're ever unsure about which one you need, just remember that graphic design is all about communication and visual design is all about appeal.

What Are the Core Components of Visual Design?

The core components of visual design include the following:

Layout:

This is the design's overall structure and how all elements are arranged. It's important to create a visually appealing layout and easy to understand. Gone are the days when designers focused strictly on the "thumb of rule" approach, and we're adhering to making wireframes, prototypes, and mockups. Although these are still important UI components, Visual design has an important place with these core components. Designers must pay special attention to what type of layout a particular website needs. Every website, mobile, or tablet has its own screen resolution, so the designers need to keep this aspect in mind as well, that their visual designs must be consistent and appealing for users of all screens. Screen resolution or screen size is an important aspect of responsive web design. The screen resolution depends on the viewing device and can be measured in pixels. Therefore when designing an app or website, it's important to consider how the layout will change based on the screen resolution.

Color:

Color is one of the most important aspects of visual design. It can be used to convey emotions, set the tone of a piece, and attract attention. When choosing colors for a design, it's important to consider the meaning of each color. For example, red is often associated with energy and passion, while blue is associated with trust and stability. The proper use of color can make a big difference in a design's overall look and feel.

An example of this is the use of dark colors vs. light colors. Dark colors tend to be more formal and serious, while light colors are more friendly and approachable.

In 2015, Google updated its logo to a more colorful and simplified design. The new logo features a sans-serif typeface and a set of four colors that can be used in any combination. The main reason for the change was to create a more modern and flexible logo that could be used across different devices and platforms. If you see any website, book, packaging, etc., that has multiple colors - they have used color combination, which is an important aspect of visual design.

Tip:
Try to use 2-3 colors in your design, as too many colors can be overwhelming. Also, make sure to use colors that complement each other.

Typography:
Typography is the art and technique of arranging type to make written language legible, readable, and appealing when displayed. The arrangement of type involves selecting typefaces, point size,

line length, leading (line spacing), letter-spacing (tracking), and kerning (pairing of letters). Good typography can greatly affect a design's overall look and feel. Fonts that are too small or have poor contrast can be hard to read, while fonts that are too large can be overwhelming. The best designs use a combination of different fonts to create visual interest and hierarchy. For example, a site might use a sans-serif font for the body text and a serif font for headings.

Airbnb is a popular travel site that uses a combination of sans-serif and serif fonts to create visual interest and contrast. The sans-serif font is used for the body text, while the serif font is reserved for headings and subheadings. This makes the site easy to read and navigate.

Tip:

Use typography to create hierarchy and contrast in your design. This helps to make the information easy to read and understand. For instance, you might use a large, bold font for headings and a smaller, regular font for body text.

Images:

Images are another important aspect of visual design. They can be used to add depth and interest to a design and communicate a message. When choosing images for a design, it's important to consider the mood and tone you want to set. An image is worth a thousand words, so make sure you choose wisely! Poorly chosen images can make a design look unprofessional and amateurish.

When choosing an image for your website or application, be sure to consider the following:

- **File size**: Large images can take a long time to load, which can frustrate users.

- **Resolution**: Images should be high-resolution so they look sharp on all devices.

- **Copyright**: Be sure you have the right to use any images you include in your design.

Slack. The popular workplace messaging app uses images extensively in its design. The images are used to add personality and flair, as well as to communicate messages. For example, the image of a cat on the login screen is used to communicate that Slack is a fun and friendly app. The image of a laptop on the home screen is used to communicate that Slack can be used on any device. This helps to create a visual design that is both appealing and easy to use.

Button Style:

Buttons are an important element of interactivity. They can be used to trigger actions, such as submitting a form or opening a menu. When designing buttons, it's important to consider the size, shape, and color. Using a particular button style can also help improve the field's usability. For example, using a button style that is easy to tap on mobile devices can make it easier for users to input data. Button style also helps to create a certain look and feel for the design. For instance, a button style that is modern and sleek can convey a more sophisticated look, while a button style that is playful and fun can convey a more youthful look. Opting for a particular button color can also help to create a certain look and feel. A bright color can convey a more energetic look, while a dark color can convey a more serious look.

Iconography:

Iconography is the use of icons in a design. Icons are simple graphical symbols that can be used to represent different concepts or ideas. In design, icons are often used to represent different actions, such as "add" or "delete." Icons can be used to add visual interest to a design and to make it more user-friendly. For example, using icons can help users quickly identify the different areas of a website or app.

When it comes to visual design, there are a few key things to keep in mind. First, choose colors that complement each other and convey the right mood for your project. Second, pay attention to typography and be sure to use fonts that are easy to read. Finally, don't forget about imagery! Images can help to add depth and interest to your design.

What Is a Style Guide?

A style guide is a document that provides guidelines for the style and format of a design. Style guides can be used for various purposes, such as ensuring consistency across a team or different products. They can also be used to define the look and feel of a brand. A style guide typically includes information on things like typography, color palette, iconography, and layout.

Creating a Style Guide:

When creating a style guide, it's important to consider the guide's purpose and who will be using it. Style guides can be created for a variety of different audiences, such as designers, developers, or clients. It's also important to consider the format of the guide and how it will be used. For example, a style guide might be created as a PDF document, or it might be an online tool that can be used to generate code snippets.

Core Components of a Style Guide:

A style guide typically includes information on things like typography, color palette, iconography, and layout. Depending on the audience and purpose of the guide, it might also include information on things like voice and tone or branding.

- **Grid:**

A grid is a system of rows and columns that are used to organize content. Grids can be used for a variety of different purposes, such as organizing text or images. When using a grid, it's important to consider the size and placement of elements.

Grids are a helpful way to create structure in a design. They can be used to segment content, make it easier to scan, and improve the overall legibility of a design. When creating a grid, it's important to consider the content that will be placed within it and the purpose of the grid. For example, if you're creating a grid for an e-commerce site, you'll need to consider things like product image sizes and placement.

- **Hierarchy:**

Hierarchy is the way in which elements are arranged in relation to one another. It's important to consider hierarchy when designing, as it can affect how easy it is for users to understand and use a design. There are a variety of ways to create hierarchy, such as using size, color, or spacing.

Hierarchy is a way of organizing content so that the most important information is given prominence. When creating a hierarchy, it's important to consider the most important information and how best to communicate that to the user. For example, designing a website might use size and color to create a hierarchy within the navigation menu.

- **Templates Sample:**

A template is a pre-designed layout that can be used to create a design. Templates are often used as a starting point for creating a custom design. Many templates are available for download online or can be created from scratch using a design tool like Photoshop or Illustrator.

When choosing a template, it's important to consider the purpose of the design and the audience. For example, if you're designing a website for a business, you might want to choose a template that includes space for a logo and contact information. If you're designing an e-commerce site, you'll need to consider things like product image sizes and placement.

Other considerations include typography, logo, color scheme, etc.

Practical Exercise:

Now that you know all about visual designing, sitemaps, and prototypes, let's notch up our UX game a bit and design our e-commerce page.

For this purpose, I made a wireframe of the home page of our e-commerce website. It is not the complete home page. The purpose is to show you the layout, color contrast, icons, navigation, buttons, logo, and just overall visuals of the website.

1. A simple logo that I created using *Canva*.

2. You see this icon a lot on websites. It's an *"account"* icon. It's a good usability function to have it on the home page.

You need to make it easy for your users to sign in. They can easily see it on the main home page.

3. Then we have the search bar right beside the account icon, which is another usability function.

4. Like all other e-commerce websites, there's a cart displayed in the top right corner of the website.

5. Remember the sitemap? Remember the primary placeholders or the level 1 placeholders in the map. Well, they are the main pages of this e-commerce website.

6. See the images. What do they tell you about our store? Yup. That it is a men's and women's fashion shop. No rocket science here.

7. Then we have the shop now button, that will take you to a page where you can choose your preferred category(men or women)

8. See the color contrast. As you can see, I have chosen some pastel pallets. What does this tell you about the website? Well, it conveys that this e-commerce shop is a fun, bold, modern fashion shop. You won't find dull and boring clothes here.

9. What about the layout? What layout can you make out from the pictures?

10. What about the typography? Although I used Roboto and simple fonts available on proto.io, I'd recommend you guys actually choose a couple of fonts that are consistent throughout their web pages.

Now that you understand the basics of visual design, it's time to put your knowledge into practice. In this exercise, you'll be creating a style guide for a fictional company.

Your task is to choose your style guide for this same e-commerce shop. And make the home page according to the layout we made in chapter 3.

For this, you may take help from these points:

1. Choose a name and logo for your company.

2. Create a color palette for your company. Include both primary and secondary colors.

3. Choose two fonts that will be used for your company's branding. One should be used for headlines and the other for body copy.

4. Select an icon or symbol that will go on the main home page.

5. Decide on the overall layout of your style guide. This should be the main home page only.

6. Include all of the elements from your company's style guide in your final design. Make sure to use the colors, fonts, and icons that you chose earlier.

7. Share your style guide with someone else to get feedback. How does it look? Is anything missing? What could be improved?

8. Make any necessary changes to your style guide based on the feedback you received.

9. Once you're happy with your final style guide, save it in a format that can be easily shared with others. This could be a PDF document or an HTML file.

Chapter 6

The USER in the UX Universe

Outline of this chapter:

- Identifying your user

- Analyzing user needs

- Prioritizing your user

- What is a user persona?

- Why should I create a user persona?

- User segmentation

UI is the saddle, the stirrups, & the reins. UX is the feeling you get being able to ride the horse.— Dain Miller

There is a reason UX is called **user experience**. *It revolves around the user*. And not just any user; your targeted user. Without input from your user, you can't design something that appeals to everyone. There are just too many people in the world with different wants, needs, and perspectives. So when you're designing your app, website, or product, you need to focus on your target user. Trust us; they matter a lot.

You need to understand as much as possible about your target users in order to design a good user experience for them. This includes understanding their needs, wants, and motivations. It also includes understanding what they would find helpful or confusing about your product or service. When you understand your user, you can be assured that your design will be created with their needs in mind. This helps to create a better user experience and can make the difference between success and failure for your product.

When it comes to UX/UI design, make sure that you take the time to understand your user. This is absolutely essential. Take as much time as you need and do as much research as the project requires. Basically, you need to put yourself in the user's shoes and think about what they would want from the product. This means taking into account their needs, wants, and desires. Only then can you create a design that will truly meet their needs.

Identifying Your User:

The first step in making the best UX/UI designs is to identify your target user. This can be done by creating a *user persona*. A user persona is a fictional character that represents your target user. This persona should include information such as the user's age, gender, location, occupation, and interests. Once you have created a persona, you can use this to help guide your design decisions. We'll come to making user personas later on in the chapter, but before that, you need to ask yourself these important questions when identifying your users.

1. Who are they?

2. What do they want?

3. How can you help them?

4. What are their pain points?

5. What motivates them?

For example, if you are designing a social media app, your target users might be teenagers who want to stay connected with their friends. They would be motivated by the need to communicate and share information with others. Their pain points might be dealing with bullies or feeling left out. As a designer, you can help them by creating a safe and secure platform for them to use.

Nike+ is a fitness app that allows users to track their progress and set goals. The app was designed with the needs of the user in mind. Nike+ understood that its target users were people who were interested in staying fit and healthy. They also knew that these users would be motivated by the need to see results and improve their fitness levels. As a result, Nike+ was designed to be easy to use and understand. It also allowed users to track their progress and set goals. This helped to create a better user experience and ensured that users were more likely to continue using the app.

Put Yourself in the Shoes of Your Target User

Analyzing user needs:

After you have identified your target user, the next step is to analyze their needs. This can be done by conducting user research. User research involves talking to users, observing them, and looking at data about them. This research will help you understand what they want from the product and how you can best meet their needs. For instance, if you are designing an e-commerce website, you might want to look at user data to see what pages they visit most, what products they are interested in, and what their buying habits are. This information can then be used to design a more user-friendly website that meets their needs.

Nike is a perfect example of a company that understands its target user and designs its products with them in mind. Nike's target user is the athlete. Nike designs its products with the needs of athletes in mind. This includes everything from the material used to the way the product fits. Nike also offers customization options for its products so that athletes can get a perfect fit. This attention to detail sets Nike apart from other brands and has helped them become one of the most successful companies in the world.

Prioritizing your user:

Once you have identified and analyzed your target user, the next step is to prioritize their needs. This can be done by creating a **user journey map**. A user journey map is a visual representation of a user's steps when using your product. This map can help you to identify where there are bottlenecks or pain points in the user experience. It can also help you see where to add value for the user. For example, if you notice that users are having difficulty finding products on your website, you could add a search bar or filters to make it easier for them to find what they are looking for.

Creating a user journey map:

1. Identify the steps that your persona takes

2. Determine where there are bottlenecks or pain points

3. Find ways to add value for the user

4. Use this map to improve the user experience.

Airbnb is a great example of a company that puts its users first. When designing their product, they put themselves in the shoes of their target user and thought about what they would want from the experience. As a result, they created a platform that is easy to use and meets the needs of their users. Airbnb also offers a wide range of customization options so that users can find the perfect listing for their needs. This attention to detail has made Airbnb one of the most popular travel websites in the world.

So now that you know how to find your ideal users and how to actually prioritize them let's move on to an important factor in user research. It is called user persona. I know another buzzword. But is it? Corporates and big forms utilize this method to actually make products for their targeted users or customers. And this literally helps them, like a lot.

So, What Is a User Persona?

A user persona is a fictional character (think Harry Potter) representing a specific user type. Personas are used to help designers understand the goals, desires, and behavior of their target users. By creating a persona, you can better understand how your target users think and feel about your product or service.

Why Should I Create a User Persona?

Creating a user persona can help you:

Creating a user persona is one of the most important steps in the UX design process. A persona is a semi-fictional character that represents your ideal user. Personas are based on market research and help ensure that your designs are tailored to your target users' needs, wants, and behaviors.

When creating a persona, you will want to consider factors such as

- Demographics
- Lifestyle, motivations, pain points, and goals. Once you have created your persona, you can use it as a reference

point throughout the design process to ensure that your designs are user-centric.

Let us take the help of a case study to make you understand this well: You want to make a dating app, and you have researched what your target users want. Now, it's time to create personas for your users. You'll need to consider the following:

- What is their age?

- What is their gender?

- What are their interests?

- What are their dating goals?

- What are their pain points with dating?

Your user persona is a man named Tom. Tom is 25 years old, lives in New York, and is interested in finding a serious relationship. He's tired of dating apps that are full of people who are only looking for hookups. Tom wants an app to help him find someone who shares his interests and is looking for a serious relationship. By keeping Tom in mind when designing your app, you can create an experience that meets his needs and helps him find his best match. For starters, he wants a serious relationship. He's interested in intelligent women with a good sense of humor. He's fed up with the dating scene and wants to find a woman with whom he can settle down. His pain points are that he feels like he's too old to be single and tired of going on dates that lead nowhere.

By understanding your target user, you can design a product that meets their needs. In this case, you would design a dating app that helps Tom find the serious relationship he's looking for. The app would be easy to use and include features that Tom is interested in, such as intelligence and a good sense of humor.

By creating personas for your target users, you can better understand who they are and what they want from your app. This allows you to design an app that meets their needs and helps them to find the perfect match.

In this example, you saw that we took into account two key points when creating this user persona.

- The user demographics
- Their wants, motivation, and aspirations.

User segmentation:

Taking this case study further, let's now focus on what user aspects and data the design team will look at. For example, a closer look at the dating app reveals that people who use this app include the following user segments:

- Single people who are looking for a serious relationship.
- Divorced individual looking for a relationship
- People who are fed up with the dating scene and want to find a long-term partner

- People who are interested in women or intelligent men who have a good sense of humor.

- People who want to find partners according to their wants and needs.

Since Tom could not find a potential long-term partner for himself or any individual who fits his level of likeness, the design team came up with the idea of a dating app that would help Tom find his perfect match and other individuals like him. The aim was to design an app that was easy to use and navigate, with features that Tom is interested in. This included intelligence and a good sense of humor, and other features.

User type	Key needs	Functionality
Divorced	<ul><li>A divorced New York local who wants to rekindle the romance.</li><li>It has to be a potential long-term relationship or</li><li>The goal is that they need to start to want to date again and want to settle.</li></ul>	<ul><li>Show singles and divorced individuals.</li><li>No hookups.</li><li>Looking to settle down again(want to get married)</li></ul>
Single looking for a long-term relationship	<ul><li>A local who wants to look for a serious relationship.</li><li>Wants to find a partner which a promising set of abilities.</li><li>It should be a perfect match.</li><li>No hookups.</li></ul>	<ul><li>Show serious relationship</li><li>Usability</li><li>Filter out hookups</li><li>The partner should live nearby or in a filtered area</li></ul>

So here you go. We're pretty sure, by now, you know how to create a user persona. Let's give your skills a try.

Practical Task:

So for this exercise, I'd like you to create a user persona of an individual who will use our e-commerce website. I would like you to start with the very first step. Identifying your user. Go down the tunnel and, in the end, make a user profile of some potential users. Remember to keep asking yourself:

1. Who are these individuals?

2. What do they want?

3. How can you help them?

4. What are their pain points?

5. What motivates them?

Chapter 7

10 Usability Heuristics

Outline of this chapter:

- Introduction

- Need for these usability heuristics

- What are the usability heuristics?

- Practical Task

Rule of thumb for UX: More options, more problems.
— Scott Belsky,

Introduction:

User Experience is a huge and important topic in the design industry, with many different schools of thought on how to best achieve it. This is a field that is constantly evolving as our understanding of how users interact with technology grows. Google's Design Sprint is a great example of how UX research and design have evolved in recent years.

However, one thing that has remained constant is the importance of usability heuristics. Usability heuristics are guidelines that help designers create products that are easy to use and enjoyable for users.

One of the most influential models for thinking about User Experience is **_Jakob Nielsen's 10 Usability Heuristics._** These heuristics are a set of guidelines that designers can use to help them create more user-friendly products.

Google's Design Sprint is a 4-day process for rapidly prototyping and testing user flows and designs. It was developed by Google Ventures and has been used by companies like Slack, Blue Bottle Coffee, and Medium. The sprint begins with a "diverge" phase, where designers come up with as many ideas as possible. These ideas are then refined and narrowed down in the "converge" phase. In the "prototype" phase, the team creates a high-fidelity prototype of the chosen idea. This prototype is then tested with users in the "test" phase.

The goal of the sprint is to compress months of work into a week so that designers can quickly and efficiently test different ideas.

The sprint is a great example of how UX research and design have evolved in recent years. It shows how important it is to rapidly prototype and test ideas before investing too much time and resources into them.

The following is a case study of how one company, R/GA, used the Google Design Sprint method to help them rapidly prototype and test a new product idea.

R/GA is a global creative agency that specializes in digital transformation. They have worked with some of the world's biggest brands, including Nike, Beats by Dre, and Google. In 2015, R/GA was approached by a client who wanted to create a new product. The client had an idea for a wearable device that would help people with anxiety disorders. R/GA knew that they needed to move quickly to prototype the product and get it into the hands of users for testing. They also knew that the product needed to be designed with UX in mind from the very beginning.

To do this, R/GA used the Google Design Sprint method. These allowed them to rapidly prototype the product and get it into the hands of users for testing within a matter of days.

Why Is There a Need for These Usability Heuristics?

Applying usability heuristics can help you improve the overall quality of your product and make it more user-friendly. By adhering to these guidelines, you can avoid common design mistakes and create a better experience for your users.

Let us now discuss each heuristic with an example and a real-world case study so that things are very clear to you at the end of this chapter.

1. Visibility of System Status:

The system should always keep users informed about what is happening through visual cues, verbal feedback, or both. Think of it like this, would users be able to tell what is happening if the power went out and they could only rely on the visual cues from the product? If not, then the visibility of system status is poor. For instance, the progress bar that appears when you're copying files from one location to another is an example of good visibility of system status. Another example is when a website shows a spinning wheel to indicate that it is loading. By showing the user the system's current status, you are making things easy for them and enhancing their UX as well.

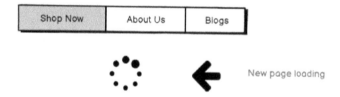

New page loading

2. Match Between the System and the Real World:

The system should use language and concepts that users are familiar with. For instance, if you're designing a website for a school, using terms like "homework" and "class" would be more appropriate than using terms like "tasks" and "groups." Also, the system should be designed in a way that is consistent with users' mental models. For example, if you're designing a website for a hotel, the user should be able to easily find the "book a room" button.

You have probably seen a recycled bin on windows and iOS desktops. It is quite familiar with how we use dust bins in real life. So a user easily knows and can locate this recycle bib to delete tier stuff from their computers and mobile phones.

Google has done an amazing job of keeping its interface clean and simple. They use common terms that users are familiar with, and they design their pages in a way that is consistent with users' mental models. For example, the "search" button is always in the same place, and the results are displayed in a way that is easy to understand.

3. User Control and Freedom:

Users should be able to easily undo any actions that they take in the system. They should also be able to abort any processes they no longer want to continue with. An example is the "undo" and "cancel" buttons found in many software applications. This allows users to feel in control of the system and prevents them from accidentally taking action that they may not be able to undo.

Microsoft Office suite includes a number of features that allow users to easily undo their actions, including the "undo" button, the "track changes" feature, and the "save as" feature. These features give users a high degree of control over their work and prevent accidental data loss.

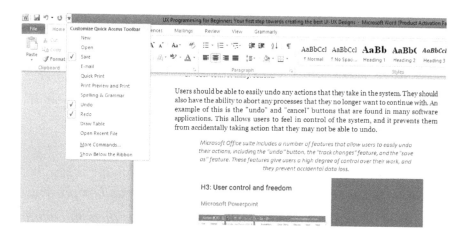

4. Consistency and Standards:

Consistency is important for usability because it helps users feel more comfortable with your product and makes it easier to use. When you're consistent with things like terminology, navigation, and design elements, users will be able to better understand and use your product. For example, if you use the same term for a button on one page and a different term for the same button on another page, users will be confused. However, if you're consistent with your terminology, users will know what to expect and be able to use your product more easily.

5. *Error Prevention:*

The system should be designed to prevent users from making mistakes. For example, if a website has a form that needs to be filled out, the form should be validated before the user submits it. This will prevent the user from accidentally entering invalid data.

The Google Search engine is designed to prevent users from making mistakes when entering their queries. For example, if a user misspells a word, the search engine will suggest the correct spelling. This helps reduce the number of errors that users make and makes the search engine more efficient.

Another example of this is the "Are you sure?" dialogue box that appears when users try to delete a file. This dialogue box prevents users from accidentally deleting files, and it allows them to cancel the action if they have changed their minds.

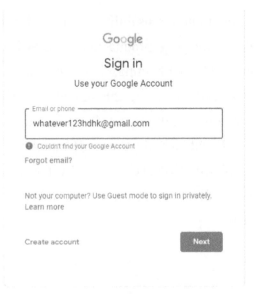

6. Recognition Rather Than Recall:

The system should be designed in a way that allows users to easily recognize the options that are available to them, rather than having to remember them. For example, if a website has a search function, the search box should be prominently displayed on every page. This will allow users to quickly and easily find the search box when they need it. For instance, Microsoft Word can save your recent files, and you can easily view the file you were working on in the recent section. In case your pc or laptop shuts off unexpectedly while you are working on a file, you can still locate it in the main software interference.

Google search engine prominently displays the search box on every page of the website. The goal is to help the user easily find what they are looking for without having to remember where it is located. If a website has a search form, the form should be clearly labeled with the word "search". This will help users to find the form quickly and without difficulty.

Ticket booking websites such as Ticketmaster also follow this design principle. The search box is prominently displayed on the homepage, making it easy for users to find and use the search function. Each function is displayed in a separate box on the homepage, which allows users to quickly and easily find the function they need.

Facebook's website is designed so that users can easily find the different functions that are available to them. For example, the "home" button is prominently displayed on the top of every page, and the "profile" button is also clearly labeled. This makes it easy for users to navigate the website and find the information they are looking for.

7. Flexibility and Efficiency of Use:

The Interface should be flexible enough to allow users to easily complete tasks in the shortest amount of time possible. The system should let a novice user perform basic tasks without difficulty while also allowing more experienced users to complete tasks quickly and efficiently. A great example of a system that is flexible and efficient to use is the Amazon website. The website allows users to quickly find the products they are looking for and provides tools that allow users to compare prices and find the best deals. A system that is not flexible and efficient to use would be a website that does not allow users to search for products or requires users to fill out long forms to purchase items.

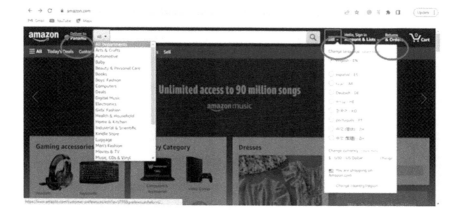

8. Aesthetics and Minimalist Design:

The system should be designed in a way that is aesthetically pleasing to the user. The design should be simple and uncluttered so that users can easily find what they are looking for. In addition, the system should use colors and other visuals that are pleasing to the eye. Google is a great example of a company that uses aesthetics and

For example, if a website has a search function, the search results should be displayed as soon as the user enters their query. This will help save time and make the website more efficient.

Google is a great example of flexibility and efficiency. At first glance, you can see that the design is simple and aesthetically pleasing. You will find your Google accounts in the top right corner. No need to go elsewhere or click extra buttons. Google offers it all on its main screen. The search results are displayed as soon as the user enters their query. This makes it easy for users to find what they are looking for without having to scroll through long lists of products.

9. Help Users Recognize, Diagnose, and Recover From Errors:

The system should be designed in a way that helps users to recognize, diagnose, and recover from errors. For example, if a user enters an invalid password, the system should display an error message that is easy to understand. The system should also provide instructions on how to recover from the error. A great case study of how to help users recognize, diagnose, and recover from errors on the Facebook website. When a user enters an invalid password, the system displays an error message that is easy to understand. The message also provides instructions on how to recover from the error.

10. Help and Documentation:

The system should be easy to learn and use, even for users who are not familiar with it. Documentation should be clear and concise, and it should be easy to find help when needed. The system should provide help to the user in case of a hurdle. Always provide information that may help the user overcome this hurdle.

Practical Exercise:

Your job is to search websites and apps and see if you can find these usability heuristics on these mediums. Make a list of what can be improved and how would you, as a UX Designer, could enhance it. For plus points, make sketches or prototypes.

Chapter 8

17 Points We Wish
We Knew about UX

Outline of this chapter:

- Know your users

- Keep up with the latest trends

- Make sure your designs are user-friendly and intuitive

- Usability

- Visual designs

- Micro-interactions

Every great design begins with an even better story.
- Lorinda Mamo

With growing technology trends, UX too has grown and changed immensely in the past decade. There are new trends and styles that one needs to keep up with in order to remain at the top of their games. How we interact with systems is forever changing, which is why many companies and brands have separate departments, teams, and budgets for finding new ways to stay ahead of their competitors.

We are at the finish line of our 1st phase of the book. We are almost done with the, let's say-technical, stuff part. In the nest phase, you will get to see some hand son activity regarding UX/UI. But for the last chapter, we will be jotting down some points that are really important to remember when making UX designs.

With that in mind, here are 17 things you can do to make sure you're always ahead of the curve.

Understand Your Users and Their Needs

This is the foundation of good UX. If you don't understand your users, you can't design anything that will be truly useful for them. Always listen to what your user has to say. Make the whole user experience simple and easy for them. Jot down every point that comes out of their mouth. Do your proper research on user profiling. This is your goal. To take them on an excellent user journey that they will thoroughly enjoy. According to author Jared Spool "If we want to design products that delight users, we need to understand three core things about them: their needs, their tasks, and their mental models." You cannot design a great user experience without understanding these three things. For instance, if you're designing a website, you need to understand what your users are trying to accomplish on the site and their mental model for how the internet works. Only then can you design something that will truly meet their needs. In our previous chapters, we discussed user profiling and making user personas. If you haven't done that yet, now would be a good time to go back and do it.

Keep up with the Latest Trends:

As mentioned before, UX is constantly evolving. New technologies and approaches are constantly emerging, so staying on top of the latest trends is important. This will help you understand what's new and how it can be applied to your work. A great way to do this is to follow UX-related blogs and websites, such as uxdesign.cc, Smashing Magazine, and A List Apart. You can also attend conferences and meetups or even join an online community such as the UX Stack Exchange. Due to technological advancements, it's important to keep up with the latest trends to maintain a competitive edge and ensure that your designs are current. The famous brand Nike is a great example of a company that does this well. Nike is always on the cutting edge of new technologies, and its website and mobile app are constantly being updated with the latest features.

Make Sure Your Designs Are User-Friendly and Intuitive

This is another important point to keep in mind. Even if your designs are user-centered, they won't be effective unless they're also user-friendly and intuitive. In other words, users should be able to figure out how to use your design without difficulty. They should also feel comfortable using it. This can be achieved through consistent layout, clear labels, and helpful cues. The famous usability expert Jakob Nielsen once said, "Users spend most of their time on other sites. This means that users prefer your site to work the same way as all the other sites they already know." So make sure your designs are familiar and easy to use. A great example of this is Amazon's shopping cart. It's designed to be familiar and easy to use, so users feel comfortable using it even if they've never used Amazon before.

Always Think in Terms of Usability

Will your design be easy and intuitive for users to navigate? You need to pay extra attention to common usability issues and design accordingly to avoid any confusion. For instance, use clear and concise labels, use icons or other visuals to represent actions, and make sure buttons are big enough and easily clickable. Ask yourself these questions while you design: what would make this task easier for the user? What could make this more intuitive? Remember your user's needs should always be at the forefront of your mind.

Pay Extra Attention to the Visual Design

The visual design is an important part of the user experience, so make sure you're giving it the attention it deserves. Consider things like the color scheme, imagery, and layout when working on the visual design of your site or app. Visual design can greatly impact the overall user experience, so don't underestimate its importance. For example, if you're designing a site for a luxury brand, the visual design should reflect that. The overall aesthetic, font, color, and icons should convey the message or the services the brand is offering.

According to a survey by Adobe, "52% of respondents said bad visual design is a bigger turnoff than a bad

copy." This just goes to show how important visual design
is to the user experience.

Microinteractions

Microinteractions are small details that can greatly impact the overall user experience. They're often used to give users feedback, such as a notification sound when they receive a new message. Microinteractions can also be used to add an element of fun or gamification to your site or app. whatever their purpose, make sure you're using micro-interactions thoughtfully and sparingly – too many can be overwhelming and distracting.

A good example of this is the "like" button on Facebook.
When you click it, you get a small pop-up notification that
says, "You liked this." This micro-interaction gives the
user feedback and makes the experience more engaging
and enjoyable.

Keep It Simple and Classy

Simplicity is key. This principle applies to all aspects of life, especially in UX design. Users don't want something complicated – they want something that's easy to use and understand. So always ask yourself if there's a simpler way to do things. If there is, go for it. A simple and classy design is always better than a complicated and cluttered one. For example, take a look at the websites of Google and Apple. They're both clean and minimalistic, and they're easy to use. That's because they've been designed with simplicity in mind.

Be Consistent

Inconsistency can be one of the most significant usability issues. Users should be able to easily understand your product or service, and that's much harder to do if things are all over the place. Try to create a consistent style throughout your design, from the colors you use to the way you format text. Consistency will make your product or service much easier to use.

You may have heard of Google's Material Design guidelines, which provide a set of rules that designers can follow to create a consistent style. The guidelines cover everything from typography to iconography. By having a uniform structure, you can create a much better user experience.

Think like a User

One of the most important things you can do as a UX designer is to think like a user. Put yourself in their shoes and try to see things from their perspective. What are their needs and wants? What are their pain points? How can you make their experience better? By thinking like a user, you'll be able to design much better solutions that meet their needs.

Get Feedback Early and Often

Feedback is essential in the design process. It allows you to validate your ideas and ensure that you're on the right track. Try to get feedback from as many people as possible, including your target audience, friends, family, and colleagues. The sooner you get feedback, the better; it's much easier to make changes early on in the process than it is later.

Be Aware of Common Usability Issues

Usability issues are problems that make it difficult for users to use a product or service. They can be caused by anything from lousy design to technical errors. Some common usability issues include confusing navigation, unresponsive buttons, and slow loading times. It's essential to be aware of these issues to avoid them in your designs. For example, make sure your website is easy to navigate and that all the buttons are responsive.

Keep Updating Your Content

The world of technology is ever-changing, so your content needs to be updated regularly to ensure it is accurate and relevant. Keep up with the latest trends and developments so you can provide accurate information to your users. Your content should reflect the latest changes in the industry. This will show that you're keeping up with the latest industry changes and developments. This will reflect positively on you as a designer and put you ahead of the competition. For instance, if you're writing a blog post about the latest trends in UX design, make sure to include the most recent changes. This will show your readers that you're up-to-date on the latest industry trends. Apart from this, you need to have outstanding content, to begin with. Content is king when it comes to UX design. Your content should be well-written, accurate, and relevant to your users. It should also be engaging and easy to read. Remember, your content is what will keep users coming back to your site or app, so make sure it's worth their while.

Offer Solutions

As a UX designer, part of your job is to solve problems. When you're writing content, make sure to offer solutions to common issues that users face. This will show that you deeply understand user needs and how to address them. For instance, if you're writing a blog post about how to design a better user flow, make sure to include tips and tricks that users can implement. Put your thinking hat on and offer solutions that are innovative and helpful.

Follow Usability Heuristics

As mentioned before, usability heuristics are a set of guidelines that help ensure a good user experience. When creating your content, make sure you follow these guidelines to ensure that users have a positive experience. Usability heuristics include things like "**visibility of system status**" and "**match between system and the real world**". With these key components in mind, you can create useful and user-friendly content.

Be Patient

Rome wasn't built in a day. Creating a great user experience takes time, effort, and patience. Don't expect to get it right on the first try; iteration is key. Be prepared to put in the work and make changes along the way. Remember to take things one step at a time; eventually, you'll get to where you want to be.

Have Fun

At the end of the day, remember that you're doing what you love. Design is supposed to be fun, so don't forget to enjoy the process. Let your creativity flow, and see where it takes you. You never know what you might come up with.

Don't Be Afraid to Fail

Failure is inevitable in any creative endeavor. But don't let it stop you from trying new things. Embrace failure and use it as a learning opportunity. Every time you fail, you'll learn something new that will help you be a better designer. Did you know that some of the most successful people in the world are also some of the biggest failures? That's because they've learned to embrace failure and use it as a stepping stone to success.

So those are our 17 tips for becoming a better UX designer. We hope you found them helpful! Keep these things in mind as you continue your journey in the world of UX, and we're sure you'll be at the top of your game in no time.

PHASE 2

Chapter 9

UX Programming
through HTML and CSS

What we'll discuss in this chapter:

- What is HTML?

- What is CSS?

- Html As a designing tool for UI

- HTML elements

- Practical task

> *Design is intelligence made visible."*
> *-- Alina Wheeler*

Introduction:

In this chapter, we will discuss how to create an e-commerce website using UI elements. Keep in mind that this is not intended to teach you HTML or CSS. Rather we will be touching and making the UI elements using the programming languages HTML and CSS.

Although creating a complete website using these languages is out of the context of this book, it's better if you practice these languages on your own. For this practical task phase of the book, we will look at UI elements such as navigation bar, toggle switch, cart, search bar, and other features using HTML.

We will use the layout and wireframe of our website's homepage.

Numerous platforms can be used to create an online store, but for the purposes of this guide, we will focus on using HTML and CSS. With these two programming languages, you will be able to create a basic but functional website that can hopefully sell products.

In today's world, HTML and CSS are not only important toolkits but necessary ones. Every designer at least should know how to work around this toolkit. I would go as far as go and call them a must-have toolkit for every designer out there. Why?

While prototype tools such as Adobe and sketch provide fast and efficient solutions, HTML and CSS provide a browser prototype functionality. You can actually see hope your designs look running on your browser. With the introduction of Bootstrap (to learn more about Bootstrap, please go to this link), things have become very easy and amazing for visual designers. These tools offer many elements and components that make beautiful visual designs.

Another reason these programming languages should be used is that they are not static. They provide an interactive flow that can be very helpful for the designers. Plus, CSS is a great toolkit if you have started working as a visual designer or graphic designer in a company because it is still relevant today.

We hope that the present website design processes will change to become more user-focused and dynamic than they are right now.

Prototyping tools, like Silver Flows, which InVision ended up buying, will introduce a new modeling approach to designing interactive wireframes, moving away from static user flows and stories.

So, in a nutshell, HTML and CSS are essential elements for designers as a result of the current professional web developments of Dynamic UI and the escalating capability of machine learning.

A designer's existence will be made easier by strong HTML and CSS skills, which also allow them to build thoughtful user interfaces.

What Is HTML?

HTML, or HyperText Markup Language, is the standard markup language for creating web pages and web applications. HTML is used to structure the content for display on a web page, including text, images, videos, and other multimedia.

CSS, or Cascading Style Sheets, is a style sheet language used for describing the presentation of a document written in HTML or XML. CSS is used to style all the content on a web page, including the text, colors, and fonts.

Before getting your hands on the practical work, let me share some HTML tags and elements with you. These are important to know since we are developing this web page through an HTML programming language. Otherwise, it is not important to learn.

HTML Elements:

- **<!DOCTYPE html>** - This tag defines the document type of the HTML file.

- **<html>** - This is the root element of an HTML file. All other elements must be contained within this element.

- **<head>** - This element contains information about the document, such as the title and metadata. Your title basically goes within this tag.

- **<meta charset="utf-8">** - This tag defines the character set for the document. In this case, it is set to UTF-8, a universal character set supporting most languages.

- **<title>**Your Ecommerce Website**</title>** - This tag sets the title of the document, which is displayed in the browser tab.

- **<link rel="stylesheet" href="style.css">** - This tag links the HTML file to a CSS file. The CSS file is used to style the document. We will come to it later.

- **<body>** - This element contains the main content of the document.

- **<h1>**Welcome to Your Ecommerce Website!</h1> - This is a heading element. There are six heading elements, ranging from <h1> (the largest) to <h6> (the smallest).

- **<p>**This is the home page of your website.</p> - This is a paragraph element. Paragraphs are used to contain blocks of text.

- **<div class="product">** - This is a division element. Divisions are used to group elements together. In this case, the division is used to group together information about a product.

- **<img src="product.jpg" alt="Product">** - This tag inserts an image into the document. The "src" attribute specifies the URL of the image, and the "alt" attribute specifies the alternative text for the image in case it cannot be displayed.

- **<h2>Product Name</h2>** - This is a heading element. As mentioned before, there are six heading elements, ranging from <h1> (the largest) to <h6> (the smallest).

HTML Text Style Attributes

The style attribute is used to specify the CSS styles for an HTML element. Styles are usually specified in a CSS file but can also be specified inline using the style attribute.

In order to use the style attribute, you must specify at least one CSS property and value. For example:

```
<p style="color:red;">This paragraph is
red.</p>
```

The "color" CSS property is set to "red" in this example. As a result, the text within the <p> element will be displayed in red.

You can specify multiple CSS properties by separating each property and value with a semicolon. For example:

```
<p style="color:red;font-size:20px;">This
paragraph is red and 20 pixels high.</p>
```

The "color" and "font-size" properties are set in this example. As a result, the text will be red and 20 pixels high.

Let's say we want to add a yellow background color to all <h1> elements on our page. We can do this by adding the following style rule to our CSS file:

```
h1 {

background-color: yellow;

}
```

Or, we could add the style inline like this:

```
<h1 style="background-color:yellow;">Welcome
to Your Ecommerce Website!</h1>
```

HTML Text Formatting Attributes

The text formatting attribute is used to specify the format of the text within an HTML element.

Text can be formatted in a number of ways, such as **bold**, *italic*, or underlined. The text formatting attribute is used to specify the format of the text within an HTML element.

For example, to make the text within a <p> element bold, we could add the following style rule to our CSS file:

```
p {

font-weight: bold;

}
```

Or, we could add the style inline like this:

```
<p style="font-weight:bold;">This paragraph is bold.</p>
```

Similarly, to make the text within a <p> element italic, we could add the following style rule to our CSS file:

```
p {

font-style: italic;

}
```

Or, we could add the style inline like this:

```
<p style="font-style:italic;">This paragraph is italic.</p>
```

To make the text within a <p> element underlined, we could add the following style rule to our CSS file:

```
p {

text-decoration: underline;

}
```

Or, we could add the style inline like this:

```
<p style="text-decoration:underline;">This
paragraph is underlined.</p>
```

HTML Colors:

The color attribute is used to specify the color of the text within an HTML element. The color can be specified either as a hexadecimal value (e.g. "#FF0000" for red) or as a named color (e.g. "red").

For example, to make the text within a <p> element red, we could add the following style rule to our CSS file:

```
p {

color: red;

}
```

Or, we could add the style inline like this:

```
<p style="color:red;">This paragraph is
red.</p>
```

Similarly, to make the text within a <h1> element blue, we could add the following style rule to our CSS file:

```
h1 {
```

```
color: blue;

}
```

Or, we could add the style inline like this:

```
<h1 style="color:blue;">This heading is
blue.</h1>
```

To make the text within a <p> element green, we could add the following style rule to our CSS file:

```
p {

color: green;

}
```

Or, we could add the style inline like this:

```
<p style="color:green;">This paragraph is
green.</p>
```

You can also specify colors using RGB values. RGB stands for "Red Green Blue". It is a way of describing colors using a combination of these three colors.

For example, the color red can be specified as RGB(255,0,0). This means that the color comprises 100% red, 0% green, and 0% blue.

Similarly, the color blue can be specified as RGB(0,0,255). This means that the color comprises 0% red, 0% green, and 100% blue.

The color yellow can be specified as RGB(255,255,0). This means that the color comprises 100% red, 100% green, and 0% blue.

HTML Images:

The <img> element is used to add images to an HTML document. The <img> element has the following attributes:

- **src**: Specifies the URL of the image to be displayed.

- **alt**: Specifies an alternate text for the image if the image cannot be displayed.

- **Width**: Specifies the width of the image in pixels.

- **Height**: Specifies the height of the image in pixels.

The following example adds an image to an HTML document:

```
<img
src="https://www.w3schools.com/images/w3scho
ols_green.jpg" alt="W3Schools" width="104"
height="142">
```

In this example, we have used the following attributes:

- **src**: Specifies the URL of the image to be displayed. In this case, the image is located at "https://www.w3schools.com/images/w3schools_green.jpg".

- **alt**: Specifies an alternate text for the image in case the image cannot be displayed. In this case, the alternate text is "W3Schools".

- **width**: Specifies the width of the image in pixels. In this case, the width is 104 pixels.

- **height**: Specifies the height of the image in pixels. In this case, the height is 142 pixels.

- The **<img>** element is an empty element, meaning it has no closing tag.

HTML Links

The <**a**> element is used to create a hyperlink. The <**a**> element has the following attributes:

- **href**: Specifies the URL of the page the link goes to.

- **Target**: Specifies where to open the linked document.

The following example creates a link to W3Schools:

```
<a href="https://www.w3schools.com">Visit W3Schools</a>
```

In this example, we have used the following attributes:

Href: Specifies the URL of the page the link goes to. In this case, the link goes to "https://www.w3schools.com".

Target: Specifies where to open the linked document. In this case, the link will open in the current window.

HTML Headings

Headings are defined with the <**h1**> to <**h6**> tags.

<**h1**> defines the most important heading. <**h2**> defines the second most important heading, and so on to <**h6**>.

The following example shows how to use headings in an HTML document:

<html>

```
<body>

<h1>This is a heading</h1>

<h2>This is a heading</h>

</body>
```

HTML Layout Elements:

HTML web page consists of several elements that make up the web page's layout.

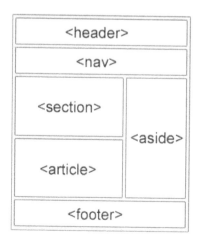

1. **The head element** - contains information about the document, such as the document's title and links to external style sheets. The header section is defined with the <head> tag.

2. **Navigation**: This element is used to navigate from one page to another. This is the bar you see on most e-commerce homepages: shop us, about us, and contact us pages. Navigation elements are defined with the <nav> tag.

3. **Section**: Section is a container element used to group related content on a web page. For example, a news article could be divided into sections for the headline, the author's name, the date, and the body of the article.

4. **Article**: The article element is used to represent a self-contained piece of content on a web page. This could be a blog post, a news article, or a product description.

5. **Aside**: Aside is a container element used to present information tangentially related to a page's main content.

6. **Footer**: Footer is a container element that is used to present information about the author of a page, copyright information, and contact details.

What Is CSS?

CSS means Cascading Style Sheets. A CSS style explains how HTML elements should appear on screens, in print, or on other devices. A great deal of work is saved via CSS. It can manage the design of several web pages simultaneously. Put simply, through CSS, we make styling appearances of the HTML element.

Let us discuss some CSS elements that will make you understand this term more easily.

Before starting our home page task, I still have a few good elements to introduce. These are very important UI elements and are a source of great User experience. I'll define them one by one and write their HTML and CSS code for you so that you can run them as well and see the results for yourself.

What Are CSS Elements?

CSS elements are the individual components of a CSS style rule. A CSS style rule is made up of a selector and a declaration block. The selector points to the HTML element you want to style. The declaration block contains one or more declarations, each consisting of a CSS property and a value.

How to add a CSS link to the HTML document?

To add a CSS link to your HTML document, you need to use the <link> element. The <link> element goes in the <**head**> section of your document.

The <**link**> element has two attributes: **rel** and **href**.

- The **rel** attribute tells the browser what kind of relationship the linked document has with the current document. The value of the rel attribute should be a stylesheet.

- The **href** attribute specifies the URL of the linked document. The href attribute's value should be the URL of your CSS file.

Here's an example:

```
<head>

<link rel="stylesheet" href="style.css">

</head>
```

In this example, the value of the rel attribute is stylesheet, and the href attribute's value is style.css. This means the linked document is a CSS file called style.css, which should be used to style the current document.

How do you write comments in CSS?

Comments in CSS are used to explain your code and can also prevent certain CSS sections from being applied.

To create a comment in CSS, you use the /* */ syntax. The browser will ignore anything between the opening /* and the closing */.

Here's an example:

```
/* This is a comment */

p {

color: red;

}
```

In this example, the comment is /* This is a comment */. The browser will ignore this comment and only apply the CSS rule p { color: red; }.

How to select an element in CSS?

To select an element in CSS, you use the selector. The selector points to the HTML element you want to style.

There are several different ways to select an element in CSS. The most common methods are by using the element's id, class, or tag name.

For example, if you have a <p> element with an id of "intro", you can select it like this:

```
#intro {

color: red;

}
```

If you have a <p> element with a class of "warning", you can select it like this:

```
.warning {

color: red;

}
```

If you want to select all <p> elements, you can do that like this:

```
p {
```

```
color: red;

}
```

Now that you know what CSS is and how it is written, let me give you a brief overview of some of the most important CSS elements that you should know as a UI designer. These elements are what we have been studying throughout the book, i.e., color, font, image size, links icon, etc. Even if you do not want to get into the depth of HTML and CSS, learning a few yet important elements won't hurt you. You never know; they may just help you with your visual design career.

How do you use colors in CSS?

To use colors in CSS, you use the color property. The color property can be used with the following values:

- a hexadecimal value, such as "#ff0000" or "#000";

- an rgb value, such as "rgb(255,0,0)" or "rgb(0,0,0)";

- An hsl value, such as "hsl(0,100%,50%)" or "hsl(0,0%,0%)".

For example, if you want to color an element red, you can do that like this:

```
element {

color: #ff0000;

}
```

How do you use Fonts in CSS?

To use fonts in CSS, you use the font-family property. The font-family property can be used with the following values:

- A specific font name, such as *"times new roman"* or *"arial"*;

- A generic font family, such as *"serif"* or *"sans-serif"*;

For example, if you want to use the Times New Roman font, you can do that like this:

```
element {

font-family: "times new roman";

}
```

If you want to use a generic sans-serif font, you can do that like this:

```
element {

font-family: sans-serif;

}
```

What is a CSS class?

A CSS class is a way of defining a set of style rules that can be applied to multiple elements.

To create a CSS class, you use the .className syntax. For example, if you want to create a class called "Intro", you would do that like this:

```
.intro {

color: red;

}
```

You can then apply that class to any element on your page like this:

```
<p class="intro">This is a paragraph with the intro class applied.</p>
```

The class name "intro" can be applied to multiple elements, and those elements will all have the same style rules applied to them.

How Does Text Formatting Work in CSS?

The following properties control text formatting in CSS:

- The font-family property, which defines the typeface to be used;

- The font-size property, which defines the size of the text;

- The color property, which defines the color of the text;

- And the text-align property, which defines how the text is aligned.

For example, the following rule would make all paragraphs on a page use the Times New Roman font, be size 16px, and be left-aligned:

```
p {

font-family: "Times New Roman";

font-size: 16px;

color: black;

text-align: left;

}
```

How do You Add Icons in CSS?

One way to add an icon in CSS is to use the background-image property. For example, if you want to add an icon of a globe, you can do that like this:

```
.icon {

background-image: url("globe.png");

}
```

Another way to add an icon in CSS is to use the font-family property. For example, if you want to add an icon of a heart, you can do that like this:

```
.icon {

font-family: "Heart";

}
```

Can You Add Icons From a Link on the Internet?

Yes, you can add icons from a link on the internet by using the background-image property. For example:

```
.icon {

background-image:
url("http://example.com/heart.png");

}
```

How do the Navigation Bars Work in CSS?

Navigation bars are created using the nav tag. The nav tag is used to create a block-level element that contains one or more links.

The links in a navigation bar can be styled using the CSS properties listed below:

- The color property, which defines the color of the text;

- The background-color property, which defines the background color of the navigation bar;

- The border property, which defines the border of the navigation bar;

- And the padding property defines the amount of space between the links and the edge of the navigation bar.

For example, the following CSS rule would make all navigation bars have a black background color, white text, and a 1px solid black border:

```
nav {

    background-color: black;

    color: white;

    border: 1px solid black;

}
```

Customized Checkbox and Radio Button:

Customized checkbox and radio button are HTML elements that allow the user to select one or more options from a list. The options in the list can be displayed horizontally or vertically, and each option can be given a custom value. Checkboxes and radio buttons can be styled using CSS to match the look and feel of the rest of the web page.

HTML and CSS code for a custom checkbox and custom radio button.

Custom Checkbox and Radio Buttons

☑ Checkbox 1 ☐ Checkbox 2 ☐ Checkbox 3 ○ Radio Button 1 ○ Radio Button 2 ○ Radio Button 3

You'll see this image on your web browser when you run the following code.

HTML and CSS code for a custom checkbox and custom radio button.

```
<!DOCTYPE html>
```

```html
<html lang="en">

<head>

<meta charset="UTF-8">

<link href="new1.css" rel="stylesheet">

<title>Custom Checkbox and Radio
Buttons</title>

 </head> <body>


<h1>Custom Checkbox and Radio Buttons</h1>
<!-- to add a container for the images -->



<div class="container"> <!-- this class
styles the container --> <!-- first custom
checkbox -->

<input type="checkbox" id="check1"> <label
for="check1">Checkbox 1</label> <!-- second
custom checkbox -->

<input type="checkbox" id="check2"> <label
for="check2">Checkbox 2</label> <!-- third
custom checkbox -->

<input type="checkbox" id="check3"> <label
for="check3">Checkbox 3</label> <!-- first
custom radio button -->
```

```
<input type="radio" id="radio1"> <label
for="radio1">Radio Button 1</label> <!--
second custom radio button -->



<input type="radio" id="radio2"> <label
for="radio2">Radio Button 2</label> <!--
third custom radio button -->



<input type="radio" id="radio3"> <label
for="radio3">Radio Button 3</label> </div>
</body> </html>
```

CSS code:

```
h1 {

font-size: 24px;

font-family: sans-serif;

color: black; } /* to style the container
for the checkboxes and radio buttons */



.container {

width: 500px; /* sets the width of the
container */

height: 375px; /* sets the height of the
container */
```

```
} /* to style each checkbox in the container
*/
```

```
.container input {
```

```
margin: 10px; /* adds a margin around each
checkbox */
```

```
}
```

Drop Down Menu:

A drop-down menu is a list of options from which the user can select. The options in the list are displayed in a "drop-down" style, where only one option is visible at a time. The other options will be hidden when the user clicks on an option. Drop-down menus are often used for navigation, where the user can choose from a list of pages to visit. Drop-down menus can also be used for other purposes, such as selecting an item from a list of options.

Dropdown menu

If you run the code below, you'll see this drop-down menu on your browser.

HTML and CSS code for creating a drop-down menu:

```
<!DOCTYPE html>

<html lang="en">

<head>

<meta charset="UTF-8">

<link href="new1.css" rel="stylesheet">


<title>Dropdown menu</title>


 </head> <body> <!-- to add a heading -->


<h1>Dropdown menu</h1> <!-- to add a
dropdown menu -->


<select class="dropdown"> <!-- the class
"dropdown" is used to style the box -->

<option>One</option> <!-- first option in
the dropdown menu -->

<option>Two</option> <!-- second option in
the dropdown menu -->
```

```
<option>Three</option> <!-- third option in
the dropdown menu -->

</select>


</body> </html>


h1 {

font-size: 24px;

font-family: sans-serif;

color: black;

} /* to style the dropdown box */


.dropdown {

width: 200px; /* sets the width of the
dropdown box */

height: 30px; /* sets the height of the
dropdown box */

border: 1px solid black; /* gives a border
to the dropdown box */

padding: 5px 10px; /* adds some padding
inside the dropdown box */

} /* to style the options in the dropdown
box */
```

```
.dropdown option {

color: black; /* colors the text in each
option black*/

}


.dropdown option {

color: black; /* colors the text in each
option black*/

}
```

Hover Button:

A hover button is a button that changes appearance when the user hovers over it with the mouse. Hover buttons are commonly used in navigation, where the user can see a list of options and choose one. Hover buttons can also be used for other purposes, such as displaying a menu of options when the user clicks on the button.

Hover Button

Before hovering

Hover Button

After hovering.

This element is such a good UI element. As a user, you need to be able to see if a component you are clicking actually works and what can be a better way to show this than changing the color of that button when you hover your cursor over it. Usability!

HTML and CSS code for change in color when the cursor hovers over a button:

```
<!DOCTYPE html>

<html>

<head>

<style>
```

```css
.button {

  padding: 10px 30px;

  text-align: center;

  text-decoration: none;

  display: inline-block;


  cursor: pointer;
}


.mybutton {

  background-color: #ff0066;

  color: black;
}


.mybutton:hover {

  background-color: #ff99cc;

  color: black;
}
}
</style>
```

```
</head>

<body>

<h2>Hover Button</h2>

<button class="mybutton">Click me!</button>

</body>

</html>
```

HTML code for breadcrumb navigation:

Breadcrumb navigation is a way of displaying the current location within a hierarchy. The breadcrumbs are typically displayed as a list of links, with the current location being the last link in the list. Breadcrumb navigation can help the user understand their current location within a website or application and provide an easy way to navigate back to previous locations.

Remember the layout we made back in chapter 4? Well, if you run the following code, this is what the navigation bar should look like.

Breadcrumb navigation

Shop › About › Contact › **Blog** ›

HTML and CSS code for making breadcrumb navigation:

```
<!DOCTYPE html>

<html lang="en">

<head>

<meta charset="UTF-8">

<title>Breadcrumbs</title>


<style type="text/css">


/* to give font size, weight, family, and
color to the heading */


h1 {

font-size: 24px;

font-weight: bold;

font-family: sans-serif;

color: black;

}


/* to give padding, background color, and
border radius to the breadcrumb container */
```

```
.breadcrumbs {

padding: 10px 10px 10px 20px;

background-color: lightgrey;

border-radius: 15px;

}


/* to give font size, weight, family, and
color to the breadcrumb elements */


.breadcrumbs li {

font-size: 16px;

font-weight: normal;

font-family: sans-serif;

color: black;

}


/* to display the list items in a row */


.breadcrumbs li {

display: inline-block; /* required for the
space between the list items */
```

```
}


/* to add a right arrow after each list item
*/


.breadcrumbs li::after {

content: " › "; /* to add the right arrow */

}


/* to style the last list item differently
*/


.breadcrumbs li:last-child {

font-weight: bold;

}


</style>

</head>

<body>


<h1>Breadcrumb navigation</h1>
```

```html
<!-- this is the breadcrumb container -->


<ol class="breadcrumbs"> <!-- first list
item -->

<li><a href="#">Home</a></li> <!-- second
list item with a link -->

<li><a href="#">Tutorials</a></li> <!--
third list item with a link -->

<li><a href="#">CSS</a></li> <!-- fourth
list item -->

<li>Breadcrumbs</li> <!-- fifth (and last)
list item that is not a link -->

</ol>


</body>

</html>


/* to add space between the list items */

li {

margin-right: 10px; /* adds space on the
right of each list item */

color: black; /* colors the text black */

}
```

As you can see, just like navigation, we have made a list of the navigation links. But here, CSS does the actual work. The "after" and "last_child" elements take the ">" icon after each link so that the user will know where they are currently on the website.

HTML and CSS code for drop-down when the cursor hovers:

Before the cursor hovers

After the cursor hovers

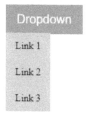

This, too, is a great UX element as it helps deliver a very seamless and easy navigation experience for the user.

Pop up Dialogue Box or Modal:

A modal is a dialogue box that pops up on the screen, usually in response to the user clicking on a button. Modals are used to display additional information or to prompt the user for input. Modals can be styled using CSS to match the look and feel of the rest of the web page.

When you run the code below, you'll see a pop window or dialogue box open like the picture shown below.

So without further ado, let us get started with our task.

Layout:

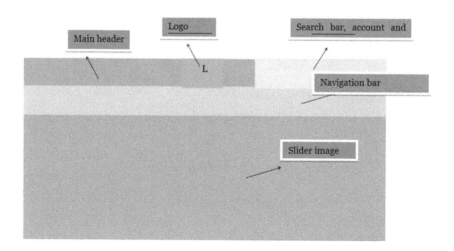

Our layout consists of these elements:

- The top bar above navigation:
- Slider image

- Search bar

- Cart

- Account log in

- Navigation bar

- Shop now buttons

We will be making these UI elements, so let's start the programming!

Okay, so I'm going to start with the top-most bar where we have our logo, search bar, cart, and account info.

Open your notepad and start typing the HTML code. This is the main home page code; therefore, we will save the file as index.html

```
<!DOCTYPE html>

<html lang="en">

  <head>

    <meta charset="utf-8">

      <link href="css.css"
rel="stylesheet">

      <div class="top-bar">

  <div class="container">

   <div class="row">

     <div class="col-6">
```

```
        <a href="#" class="logo"><img
src="C:\Users\sandh\Downloads\white.png"
alt="girl" style="width: 50px; height:
45px;"</a>

        <div class="col-6">

          <form>

            <input type="text"
placeholder="Search">

            <!--<button type="submit"><i
class="fa fa-search"></i></button>-->

          </form>

          <a href="#" class="account">My
Account</a>


          <a href="#" class="cart"><i
class="fa fa-shopping-cart"></i>
Cart</a></div>


        </div>

  </div>

      </div>

  </div>
```

Okay, so as we mentioned before, this is the top bar, and it has four components in it:

- The logo

- Search bar

- My account

- Cart

I named this complete set *top bar* and enclosed it in the "*division*" element since these elements are a complete group entwined together in the top bar.

This shows the logo that you see on the top bar. The logo is saved in my local drive, so I have given the path and set its width and height to 50 px and 45 px.

```
<a href="#" class="logo"><img
src="C:\Users\sandh\Downloads\white.png"
alt="girl" style="width: 50px; height:
45px;"</a>

Next comes the search bar

        <form>

            <input type="text"
placeholder="Search">

            <!--<button type="submit"><i
class="fa fa-search"></i></button>-->

        </form>
```

I used the form tag for the search bar since it's an input element. I have also used a button called *submit*. So once you have entered your query, you can press this button. Having this button is unnecessary since you can simply enter the *key* from your mobile phone or keypad.

Next is the account icon or link and cart icon or link. I have used a simple *link* to show these elements.

```
<a href="#" class="account">My
Account</a>

<a href="#" class="cart"><i
class="fa fa-shopping-cart"></i>
Cart</a></div>
```

You can add an icon to these classes if you like to and then add a link to that ICON OR IMAGE. Running this code will show you the following image.

The next step is to add the bar that displays a text message telling the user that they'll get 50% off on their

For this purpose I have simply used a paragraph tag

```
<p class="blink">GET 15% OFF ON YOUR FIRST
ORDER</p>
```

Interestingly you see a class labeled as "blink". To attract users to this offer, I have styled the text so that it flashes! Here is where your CSS comes in.

```
.blink {
```

```
      animation: blinker 1.5s linear
infinite;


      }

   @keyframes blinker {

      50% {

         opacity: 0;

      }
```

The blink class shows how long this animation will run and what the opacity should be. The *@keyframes* rule is used to define the animation code. The animation is created by gradually changing from one set of CSS styles to another. You can change the set of CSS styles during the animation many times.

Running this code will show us a flashing text message on a bar

```
                    GET 15% OFF ON YOUR FIRST ORDER
```

After this, we have our navigation tab. Our navigation tab consists of a shop, about us, contact us, and blog pages.

```
   <ul>

      <li><a href="default.asp">Shop</a></li>

      <li><a href="news.asp">About us</a></li>
```

```
<li><a href="contact.asp">Contact
us</a></li>

<li><a href="about.asp">Blog</a></li>

</ul>
```

For this, I have used the *ul* and *li* elements. The ul tag in HTML is used to create an unordered list. This list can contain items with bullet points, or it can be a nested list contained within another ul tag. The li tag in HTML is used to create a list item. This list item can then be contained within an ordered or unordered list. Your li tags need to be included within the ul tag. The *a href* tag defines a hyperlink. The hyperlink points to another location on the web, either on the same site or on a different site. The *href* tag is used to create links between pages on the web.

The CSS style for this HTML code is:

```
ul {

    list-style-type: none;

    height: 50px;


    overflow: hidden;

    display: block;

    margin-top: -16px;

    margin-left: 0px;
```

```css
    margin-right: 0px;

    background-color: #D790E8;

    padding: 0px;

    margin-bottom: 0px;

}

li {

  float: left;

    padding-left: 50px;

    font-size: 20px;

    font-family: serif;

    padding-top: 20px;

}

li a {

  display: block;

  margin-top:-60px;

  padding: 60px;



  color: white;

}
```

Now let's discuss each element in this code:

First, anything written in the *ul{}* block will style the complete block. The background color: *#D790E8*; this block's color is purplish. You'll see two elements that are very important to understand here: padding and margin. Padding is the space between the content of an element and the border of that element. Padding can be added to all sides of an element (top, right, bottom, and left). Padding is often used to create space around elements on a page, making them more visible and easier to interact with. For example I've written   padding: 0px;

This means that I'm giving no space between the ul's border and the content within the *Ul* element that are the links.

And if you want to give your element some space from another element, you can use the margin property. For example, I can use the margin property if I want to give a little space between the navigation bar and the outside container. You can set margin for top, bottom, left, and right

Moving on to the *li{}* block, this block specifies properties for the block of the four links. Here is an element that you need to understand, and that is the float property. Using the float attribute, an item can be set to glide to the right or left or not move at all.

Running the above code will display:

| Shop | About us | Contact us | Blog |

Now the final step here is to create the image banner. I have already made this image on Canva. You can find it here:

I have made a *Shop now* button on the image, but you can also make it separately. I'll show you how to do it.

```
<body>

<div class='header_box'>

    <div class='header'>

    <img class="myimage"
src="C:\Users\sandh\Downloads\Beige Paper
Texture Bath & Body eCommerce Web
Banner.png" alt="dd" width="100%"
height="auto"/>

    </div>

</div>

<!---->

</body>\
```

Remember the layout template we discussed. Well, the image has to be enclosed in the body. The navigation and two bars were enclosed in the head. But now we've moved to the body part. So enclose the image code in the body tags.

I have the image in a div class called "*header*"; that way, it will be easy for you to play around with this div class in whatever way we want to.

In the img class, src means the source of the file. My image has been saved in this path: *C:\Users\sandh\Downloads\Beige Paper Texture Bath & Body eCommerce Web Banner.png*. You can also add a web link here. I have set the width to a 100%, meaning the width will be displayed according to the web browser's layout.

Creating an eCommerce website can be divided into two parts: the front-end and the back-end. The front-end is what the user sees and interacts with, **while** the back-end is where all of the behind-the-scenes magic happens. In this chapter, we have discussed creating the back end. And honestly, all the magic happens here!

Final Thoughts!

By now, you should understand what UX programming is and how it can help you create better UI/UX designs. Remember that UX programming aims to make the user experience more efficient and effective. And always keep in mind the three key principles of UX programming: simplicity, consistency, and feedback.

Simplicity:

The first principle of UX programming is simplicity. This means that the user interface should be easy to understand and use. It should be free of clutter and unnecessary features. The goal is to make the user's experience as efficient and effective as possible.

Consistency:

The second principle of UX programming is consistency. This means that the user interface should be consistent across all devices and platforms. It should use the same terminology, icons, and layout on all devices. The goal is to make the user's experience as consistent as possible.

Feedback:

The third principle of UX programming is feedback. This means that the user interface should provide feedback to the user. Feedback can be in the form of error messages, confirmation messages, or simply notifications. The goal is to make the user's experience as effective as possible.

Practical Task

Keep building this web page! Add new elements to it. Remember the pencil sketch we made in chapter 2. Well, make those remaining elements in HTML and CSS.

Chapter 10

Designing Via Prototype Tools

In this chapter, we will discuss:

- The UI/UX tools

- How do UI designers design prototypes?

- HTML and CSS Vs. UI Prototype tools

- Top 10 UI tools

- Practical Task

> *Design adds value faster than it adds costs."*
> *-- Joel Spolsky, creator of Trello*

What Are UI/UX Tools?

User interface (UI) and user experience (UX) tools are software programs that help designers create websites and applications that are easy to use and provide a great user experience. UI tools focus on the look and feel of the website or application, while UX tools focus on the user's experience when using the site or app. Many different types of UI/UX tools are available, and the best one for you will depend on your specific needs.

When choosing a UI/UX tool, it's important to consider your budget, the features you need, and how easy the tool is to use. There are many great UI/UX tools on the market, so take your time to find the one that's right for you.

How Do UI Designers Design Prototypes?

There are a few things to consider when designing prototypes for UI. First, the prototype should be easy to use and understand. Second, it should be visually appealing and engaging. And finally, it should be able to convey the product or service's message clearly. To create a great prototype, UI designers need to understand design and user experience strongly. They should also be familiar with various prototyping tools and software.

Do UI Designers Need to Learn Some Programming Language to Make UI Prototypes?

No, UI designers do not need to learn how to code. However, knowing how to code can be helpful when it comes to understanding the technical aspects of prototyping and creating a working prototype. Additionally, being able to code can also make it easier to communicate with developers during the design process.

HTML and CSS vs. UI Prototype Tools: Which One Should I Go For?

There is no single answer to this question as it depends on your specific needs and preferences. If you are looking for a tool that will help you quickly create a prototype of your website or application, you might consider using a UI prototype tool. On the other hand, if you want more control over the design and development process, then you might want to use HTML and CSS. HTML and CSS are used best when you are new in the industry, or your project is small in scope. But if you have more experience, then a UI prototype tool can be a better choice as it will save you time in the long run.

Some of the most popular UI/UX tools include wireframing tools, prototype builders, design frameworks, and style guides. Wireframing tools help designers create basic layouts for their websites or applications. Prototype builders allow designers to create interactive prototypes of their designs so that users can test them out. Design frameworks provide a structure for designers to follow when creating their designs. And style guides help designers maintain a consistent look and feel throughout their website or application.

Top 10 UI prototype Tools According to US (Yes, actually, a great deal of research went into this)

As mentioned a thousand times before, Prototypes are an excellent way to quickly create a working model of your website or application. They can save you time and help you create a better user experience. Through prototypes, visual designers can explore different design options and test the feasibility of an idea. And developers can use prototypes to create a working model of an application before starting the coding process.

Many prototype tools are available on the market, and it can be hard to choose the right one for your project. To help you make a decision, we've compiled a list of the 10 best prototype tools.

1. Balsamiq Mockups

Balsamiq Mockups is a wireframing tool that allows designers to create basic layouts of their websites or applications. It offers a wide range of features and is relatively easy to use, making it a good choice for beginners. You can easily create clickable prototypes with Balsamiq Mockups.

Pros:
- Simple user interface that is easy to use
- Comes with a wide range of features
- Drag-and-drop makes it easy to create prototypes

Cons:
- The free version is limited in features

2. *Adobe XD:*

Adobe XD is a powerful tool for creating high-fidelity prototypes. It offers a wide range of features, including vector-based drawing tools, symbols, and collaboration tools. And it integrates with other

Adobe products, making it easy to create prototypes that look like the final product.

Pros and Cons of using Adobe XD:

Pros:

- Wide range of features

- Vector-based drawing tools

- Integrates with other Adobe products

Cons:

- More expensive than other prototype tools

3. InVision:

InVision is a popular tool for creating prototypes and collaborating with team members. It offers a wide range of features, including real-time collaboration, version control, and commenting. And it integrates with an extensive assortment of tools, making it easy to generate a model that looks like the actual product.

Pros and Cons of using InVision:

Pros:

- Great features

- Real-time collaboration

- Integrates with a wide range of tools

Cons:

- It can be expensive for large teams

4. *Justinmind:*

Justinmind is a scheming tool for producing high-fidelity models. It offers a wide-ranging range of features, comprising vector-based illustration tools, icons, and teamwork tools. And like other tools, it too assimilates with other plugins easy

Pros and Cons of using Justinmind:

Pros:

- Variety of features
- Variety of illustration tools
- Integrates with other Adobe products

Cons:

- More expensive than other prototype tools

5. *Moqups:*

Moqups is a quick and easy way to create wireframes and prototypes. It has a simple user interface that makes it easy to get started. And it comes with a wide range of features, including drag-and-drop, symbols, and collaboration tools.

Pros and Cons of using Moqups:

Pros:

- Simple user interface that is easy to use
- Comes with a wide range of features
- Drag-and-drop makes it easy to create prototypes

Cons:

- The free version is limited in features

6. *Mockplus:*

Similar to Moqups, Mockplus is a fast and easy way to generate wireframes, mockups, and prototypes. It has a simple user interface that makes it easy to get started. And it comes with a wide range of features, including symbols, collaboration tools, and a built-in asset library.

Pros and Cons of using Mockplus:

Pros:

- Simple user interface that is easy to use

- Comes with a wide range of features

- A built-in asset library makes it easy to find the right resources for your project

Cons:

- The free version is limited in features

7. *Axure RP:*

Axure RP streamlines the wireframing and development processes, assisting businesses in creating better digital products. It enables designers to make the advanced approach to websites and applications in resolutions ranging from low to high without writing any code.

Axure RP delivers a thorough reference mechanism in addition to everything you need to design the graphics, interactions, and organization. This tool allows constant monitoring of ideas, activities, and other crucial materials organized and available to anyone in need.

8. WebFlow

We're prejudiced with this one, but we also understand that you want a quicker and more efficient creative process, so we're here to support you.

Webflow handles two tasks at once. You can develop a functional webpage with HTML, CSS, and related Java whilst designing and producing a high-quality model. Instead of merely a prototype, you'll get the real thing.

9. Sketch

Sketch is a vector drawing and animation software that is popular among UI designers. It offers a wide range of features and is relatively easy to use, making it a good choice for both beginners and more experienced designers. Sketch also allows you to create clickable prototypes of your designs. Some con of this tool is that it can be challenging to learn if you're not familiar with vector drawing software, and it's only available for Mac.

10. Origami Studio

Facebook offered the freeware prototype platform Origami Studio after creating it as a requirement for its designers.

Origami Studio provides strong prototype capabilities for websites and mobile applications for developers who require a more complex framework. A Patch Builder, which is at the heart of Origami Studio, enables you to create logical concepts, behaviors, motions, and interactivity. Each patch serves as a quick-iterating building element for your design.

Adobe Photoshop is a widely used raster graphics editor, and for a good reason – it's fairly easy to use and offers a wide range of features. However, there are also some drawbacks to using Adobe Photoshop. One downside is that it can be expensive – the software isn't cheap, and you also need to pay for a subscription to use it. Additionally, Adobe Photoshop can be a bit overwhelming for beginners, as there is a steep learning curve. But if you're willing to put in the time to learn the ropes, Adobe Photoshop can be a great tool for UI design.

Apart from these platforms, designers also use JavaScript, HTML, and CSS to create prototypes. Some of the most popular UI/UX tools used by designers are wireframing tools, prototype builders, design frameworks, and style guides. Wireframing tools help designers create basic layouts for their websites or applications. Prototype builders allow designers to create interactive prototypes of their designs so that users can test them out. Design frameworks provide a structure for designers to follow when creating their designs. And style guides help designers maintain a consistent look and feel throughout their website or application.

When it comes to choosing the best UI/UX tool for your needs, it's important to consider your budget, the features you need, and how easy the tool is to use. There are many great UI/UX tools on

Let us start our practical task:

Go to Balsamiq.com (https://balsamiq.com/) and download the software for desktop.

Here's the link for it. https://balsamiq.com/wireframes/desktop/

After installing the software on your computer, open it. It should look like the following picture.

This is what the Balsamiq wireframe looks like.

Let us start making our first project in it. As soon as you open Balsamiq, the interface looks something like this.

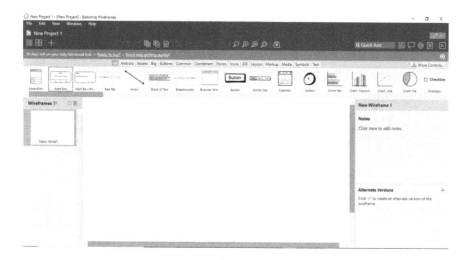

Now let me give you a brief overview of all the elements Balsamoiq provides.

At the top, you will see a bar displaying the UI element Balsamiq provides. You will find **MOST** of the UI elements that we have discussed throughout the book here. This is why I love Balsamiq. It is easy to use and provides the user with a very efficient layout and display.

Okay, as you can see, I have clicked on the "*All*" tab, which displays UI elements such as Accordion(Drop down menu or collapsible menu) and Alert box, which we discussed in previous chapters, you can see *breadcrumb* navigation.

So basically, you just have to drag these elements on your selected wireframe.

Talking about *wireframes*, Balsamiq also provides you with options to choose layouts such as mobile phone layout or desktop or web layout. Lease see the image below for a better understanding.

For our exercise, I have chosen *the browser window wireframe* layout.

Okay, so now, moving after choosing the browser window, your Balsamiq interface should look like this:

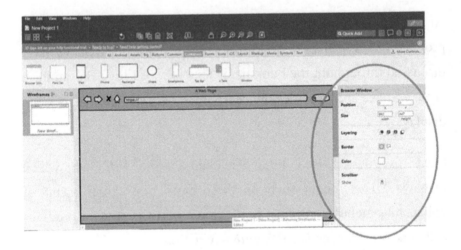

On the right-hand side, you can see the *element's* options. You can customize your chosen element from here. For example, you can change the size of the browser window wireframe or bring it forward or send it backward. You can also change the color.

Now, if you look at the sketch we made of our e-commerce homepage, there is a top bar followed by another bar flashing a text which is followed by the navigation bar and then the header image.

For the top bar that consists of a logo, search bar, account information, and cart, I selected the rectangle option from the "*containers*" bar

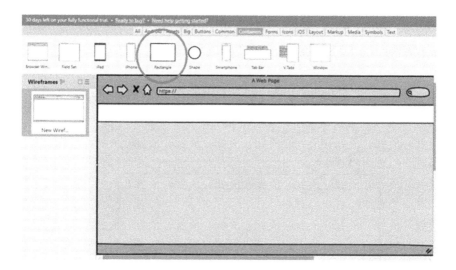

After this, I inserted the ***search bar***, the user account, and cart symbols. I also inserted the image element. If you "***double click***" the image element, you'll be able to upload an image straight from your computer in that placeholder.

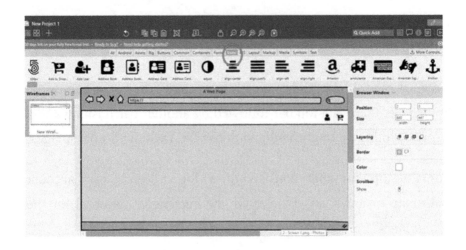

Pro tip: rather than opening an individual tab one at a time. Simply search for the UI element in the "Quick add" field.

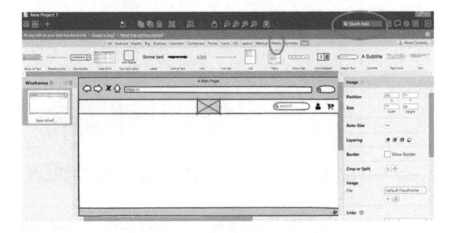

You'll find the image element from the **"*media*"** tab, but I'd rather you search it from the quick add input field.

So there you go, we have inserted our items which make up the top-most bar of our home page.

Now moving to the second bar, which contains the flashing text (we will not beading the flashing property here). Drag the rectangle element like we did with the top bar and insert the "*text*" element.

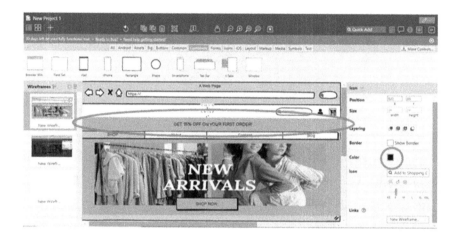

Again as you can see, I have changed the background color. You can select any color of your choice from the right side of your interface.

Now we'll come to the navigation bar. For the navigation bar, you have three options. You can choose the ***button bar*** as your placeholder for the shop, About, contact and blog links, or you can insert a link or menu bar. I have used a button bar as these look visually close to how a navigation bar looks like.

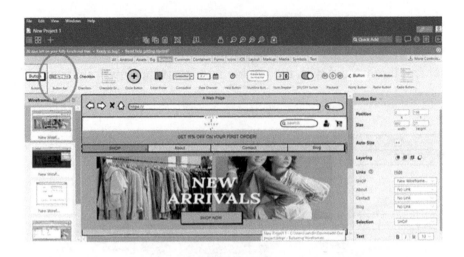

As you can see on the right side, you have information regarding the element. As our navigation bar consists of 4 web page links, the right side shows four links. Only the shop web page is linked to another wireframe. What does this mean? Well, when you'll click the chop button, you will be taken to another web page which will most probably show you the categories of the shop button, or maybe it will be a ***drop-down menu***. This is the beauty of UI Tools. You can test the system as a user.

I have uploaded the project on Google drive for you guys to use and run the prototype as well. This is the link:

https://drive.google.com/drive/folders/1z0lXrUcvJPTWCIMePHq Mtom2vxWk_6eK?usp=sharing

Anyway, back to *navigation*, so you'll simply insert the wireframes in these link placeholder so that when you click these *buttons*, you'll be taken to the next step. I will show you the next step by clicking the "*shop*" button in a while. But first, let us move to the image banner but before that, let me show you what the menu bar and link bar look like.

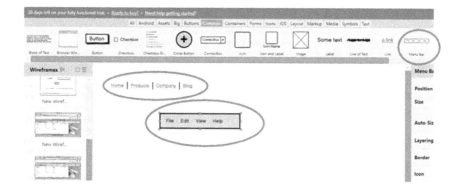

Okay, it's time for the image banner after the navigation bar. For this purpose, I simply dragged the image element and uploaded our image header, which is the main image of our home page.

After that, I inserted a button on top of this image and labeled it as shop now.

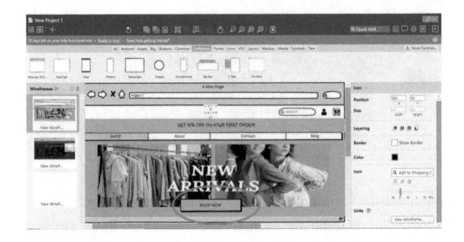

So there you go, this is the upper half of our main home page.

Now it's time to let you in on how the interaction or flow works in Balsamiq. By flow, I mean how we can navigate from one page to another or what will happen if I click the cart button.

Now, if you have ever shopped online, you know that when you click the cart button, you'll see some sort of a drop-down displaying the items you have selected. In most cases, we have the option to edit the inserted items, such as remove them or update the number of these items. Lastly, we see the option for "checkout" or simply to "continue shopping".

And when this drop-down appears, you want the user to focus only on that particular element. This is why when you shop online, you see the background blurred out, and only the drop-down item list or item menu is focused. Well, I, too, made this possible. See the image below for a better understanding.

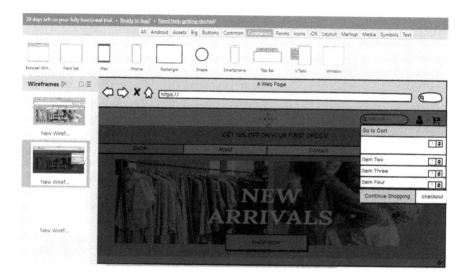

First of all, I have chosen a simple accordion element to display the items in the cart. Then I added the number stepper element in front of the *item text.*

You can search for these elements from the *quick add* or can find the *number stepper* from the button panel and the *accordion* from the layout tab.

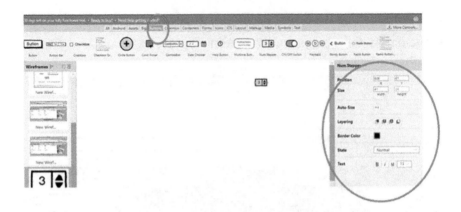

Just like any other element, you can customize the number stepper too. You can change the number or can change the color etc.

Similarly, the accordion also displays its own set of customizations. You can add links to the items in the accordion bar as well.

Okay, so back to the cart thingy. I have inserted two buttons, one for centime shopping and the other will take you to the checkout page.

Lastly, to make it all focusable and a good usability instrument, I made the background a little opaque by placing a rectangle over the elements and bringing its transparency to a low number.

Now the question here is, how do you link these two wireframes? If I click the cart button, how will I see the cart items displayed?

Well, I simply selected the *cart icon*. On the right side, you'll see the option for the *link*. Here I selected the wireframe, which contains the cart information from the link option.

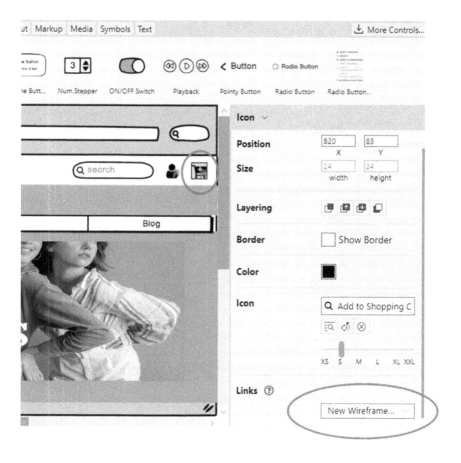

The name of the cart wireframe was ***wireframe copy 1***, so I simply selected it from the drop-down display. You'll see a red mark on the cart, which means this is a linked feature in Balsamiq and will take you to a new wireframe.

Okay, what happens if I click the "User account" symbol? I also linked it to a page. But what does this page show? Well, see the image for yourself.

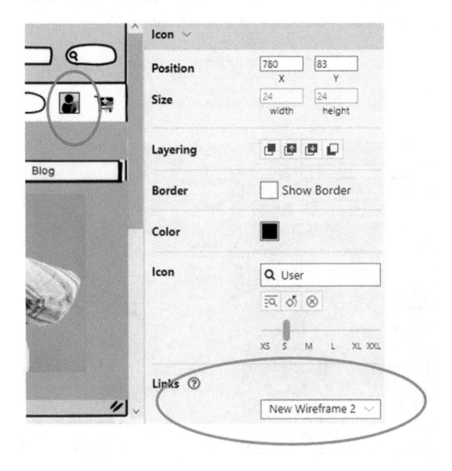

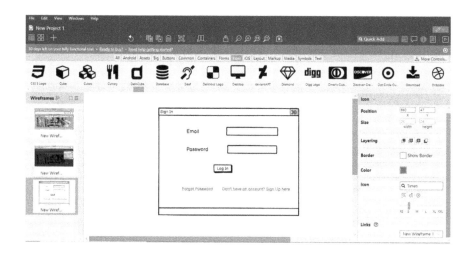

Tada! The user account icon takes you to a page that *rightfully* asks you to log in. If you're a user or haven't registered yet, you'll need to sign up, right? So there's an option for that as well. And if your user forgot his password, there should be a link that will take him to a form where they can reset the tier password. Usability! Functionality! Remember?! This is what good UX should look like.

See that little cross icon on the upper right corner of the form? Clicking it would take you back to the main home page or the page from where you logged in, although, in my opinion, there should be a cancel button since we need the user to log in or sign up. That's the purpose of this form, but let's say the user doesn't want to log in or sign up at the moment, and instead just wants to surf the shop, well why should we stop them? We should let them do whatever they want.

Now, let's say you want to shop and have decided to see what this e-commerce store offers. Obviously, you'll click the shop button.

What do you expect to see? A drop-down with all the categories for a man or a woman's apparel? Well, this is what we did.

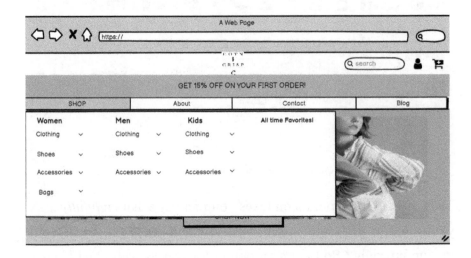

On clicking the shop button, we see a drop-down menu that displays the categories this shop offers in women's, men and kids' fashion.

Recall the sitemap we made in chapter 3. It looks something like this:

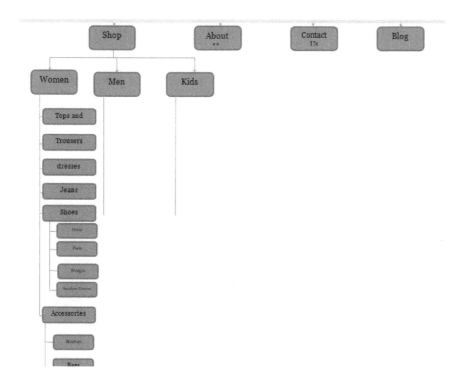

As you can see, the shop has three components, men, women, and kids.

If we further break it down, we can add further categories. Considering this sitemap, we made the drop-down of our shop link. Clicking the categories further will give us sub-categories. For example, if I click the drop-down icon in front of clothing in the women's section, I'll probably see tops and blouses, dresses, jeans, trousers, etc. let's make this sub-category in Balsamiq.

Remember that you are not creating the final product while using a Prototype tool. A prototype's purpose is to test an idea's feasibility and to gather user feedback. They are usually created quickly and are not meant to be perfect. So don't get discouraged if your prototype isn't perfect. Just keep iterating and refining until you get it right.

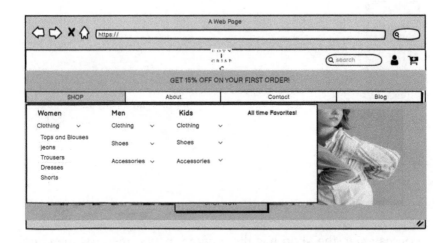

Doesn't it look awesome! Just like a real website

Well, this is it.

I'm going to leave the rest of the page to be done by your guys! And I'm sure you'll do an awesome job.

Remember to make the flow as effortlessly as possible. Go see e-commerce websites for a change and see how they work. This will give you a great idea. And lastly, but most importantly, practice, practice, and practice some more! You can only work your way around this if you practice.

Start with making prototypes on paper, then use an interactive tool such as Balsamiq. Study your audience.

Final Thoughts on UI Prototypes and Tools:

UI prototypes are a great way to quickly create your website or application prototype. They can save you time in the long run and help you create a better user experience. However, if you want more control over the design and development process, then you might want to use HTML and CSS. HTML and CSS are used best when you are new in the industry, or your project is small in scope. But if you have more experience, then a UI prototype tool can be a better choice. Balsamiq is an excellent tool for creating prototypes. It is easy to use and has a wide range of features. If you are looking for a more sophisticated tool, you might consider using Adobe XD. Adobe XD is a powerful tool that allows you to create high-fidelity prototypes. But it is also more expensive and requires a subscription. In the end, it all comes down to your specific needs and preferences. Choose the tool that best suits your needs. Thanks for reading! :)

Conclusion

Well, this is it. This is where we say goodbye. But not before we share a few final words that can really round things up for you.

The first and foremost thing to keep in mind is that UX and UI designing is really changing the way we do things these days. It is no longer acceptable for companies to provide the general public with products that do not take user experience and proper interface development into account. There will always be room for improvement of course, but the fact of the matter is, the digital world is set on "user" foundations, and it is the user who determines what works and what doesn't. So, as a programmer or designer, you need to keep this in mind, and know that what you're doing really does make a difference.

This book breaks down each and every aspect of UX and UI designing and programming to make readers like you understand how it all works. Since you are a beginner and want to be the best, I sincerely hope that this book has been of some help. Each chapter in this book takes one concept from the UX world and explains it in detail so you can apply it to your designs. No rubbish, no fluff. Simple concepts that can actually help blooming individuals like you learn these ideas easily. Every chapter in this book contains easily digestible knowledge you can apply to your work immediately.

The most important thing to remember is that practice makes perfect. The only way you're going to get better at UX design is by designing. A lot.

So what are you waiting for? Get out there and put your newfound knowledge to the test. And if you ever feel lost, don't hesitate to come back and take another read.

We wish you all the best in your journey to becoming a great UX/UI designer!

Thank you for buying and reading/listening to our book. If you found this book useful/helpful please take a few minutes and leave a review on Amazon.com or Audible.com (if you bought the audio version).

References

Marsh, J. (2016). UX for Beginners: A Crash Course in 100 Short Lessons (1st ed.). O'Reilly Media.

USER EXPERIENCE (UX) DESIGN CONCEPTS FOR MOBILE APP DEVELOPMENT COURSES. (2020). Issues In Information Systems. https://doi.org/10.48009/4_iis_2020_202-211

CareerFoundry. (n.d.). UX Tutorial 1: What Exactly Is UX Design? (Free Course). https://careerfoundry.com/en/tutorials/ux-design-for-beginners/what-is-ux-design/

Store, C. (2022). UI/UX DESIGN WIREFRAME SKETCHBOOK: Wireframes dummies Responsive Sketching Notebook For UI and UX Designers. Independently published.

Godwin, N. (2022). UX/UI DESIGN 2022 BEGINNERS TO ADVANCED USER GUIDE: The Ultimate Step by Step Guide to Mastering the UX/UI Design + Best Practices for Beginners to Intermediate and Advanced Designers. Independently published.

Buxton, B. (2007). Sketching User Experiences: Getting the Design Right and the Right Design (Interactive Technologies) (1st ed.). Morgan Kaufmann.

Lupton, E. (2017). Design Is Storytelling (1st ed.). Cooper Hewitt, Smithsonian Design Museum.

Press, Scripto Love. (2021). UX/UI Designer Notebook (White): UX/UI Design for Mobile, Tablet, and Desktop - Sketchpad - User Interface - Experience App Development - Sketchbook - . . . App MockUps - 8.5 x 11 Inches With 120 Pages. Independently published.

Allanwood, G., & Beare, P. (2019). User Experience Design: A Practical Introduction (Basics Design) (2nd ed.). Bloomsbury Visual Arts.

Vieira, J. (2019, June 11). Coding for Designers: How Much Should We Know? Toptal Design Blog. https://www.toptal.com/designers/ui-ux/designers-coding

Colborne, G. (2017). Simple and Usable Web, Mobile, and Interaction Design (Voices That Matter) (2nd ed.). New Riders.

How To Become A Self-Taught UI/UX Designer. (2022, January 5). Https://Dribbble.Com. https://dribbble.com/resources/how-to-become-ui-ux-designer

Jones, C. (n.d.). UX/UI Design 2022: A Comprehensive UI & UX Guide to Master Web Design and Mobile App Sketches for Beginners and Pros.

Books, UX/UI Designer. (2020). UX / UI Wireframe Design Sketchbook: Mobile, Tablet and Desktop templates for responsive designs with project planning. Independently published.